TRANSFORMER

A STORY OF **GLITTER**, **GLAM ROCK** & **LOVING**

SIMON DOONAN

HarperOne
An Imprint of HarperCollinsPublishers

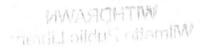

HarperCollins books may be purchased for educational, business, or sales promotional use. For information, please email the Special Markets Department at SPsales@harpercollins.com.

FIRST EDITION

Designed by Leah Carlson-Stanisic
Unless otherwise noted, photographs courtesy of the author.
Photograph on pages i and iv © Iakov Kalinin/Shutterstock.

Library of Congress Control Number: 2022944157

ISBN 978-0-06-325951-5
ISBN 978-0-06-329539-1 (ANZ)

22 23 24 25 26   LSC   10 9 8 7 6 5 4 3 2 1

THIS BOOK IS DEDICATED TO THE MEMORY OF LOU REED, HOLLY WOODLAWN, CANDY DARLING, AND JACKIE CURTIS. MAY YOU WALK ON THE WILD SIDE FOR ETERNITY.

Contents

Biddie (in bra) and me, snapped by Mum, circa 1960, and observed by
sister, Shelagh, the only person not wearing Mum's clothes.

Introduction

In the 1960s I developed a habit of mincing round the backyard in the style of the Ballets Russes with a dollop of Carmen Miranda. My non-mincing hours were spent gagging over fashion mags filled with startling shots of models du jour Jean Shrimpton and Twiggy. On rainy days my best friend and I busied ourselves putting on fashion shows in my attic, wearing my mum's clothes. I was not out. Nobody was. Being out wasn't a thing back then.

Sensing there might be a pansy among the begonias, Terry Doonan, my dad, a veteran of the Second World War, swung into action. All the adult men of my youth had fought in either the First or the Second World Wars. They were straightforward. They were butch. Some had undiagnosed PTSD and were drunken and violent. My dad was a rather nice chap.

One Sunday afternoon Terry surprised me in my drag atelier, which, as chance would have it, offered a fantastic view of Reading Gaol, as in Oscar Wilde, as in *The Ballad of Reading Gaol*. Yes, the very institution where Oscar Wilde was incarcerated, having been convicted of gross indecency, which sounds very louche and Lou Reed–ish. Without ever addressing my sexuality directly, my dad delivered a short speech that was clearly intended to put the kibosh on my emerging flamboyance.

"Homosexuals lead lonely lives. They get beaten up and thrown in jail, just like Oscar Wilde. They get blackmailed too. They often commit suicide."

I have no recollection of responding. The coming out process did not exist back then. Most likely there was an excruciating Pinter-esque silence during which we stared at the Victorian jail, wreathed in noxious vapors belching from the adjacent Huntley & Palmers biscuit factory. My mother once had applied for a job at H & P and was told that they would have to pay her less because she was Irish. Needless to say, she told them where they could shove their buttered shortbread triangles.

In cities and villages and tenements, from Scranton to Glasgow, parents were attempting the exact same Terry Doonan scared-straight tactic in the hope that their kids might avoid the brutal outcomes that ruined so many lives. Some parents, like Mr. Doonan, used words. Some used violence. Some used bribery. Lou Reed's parents opted for eight weeks of electric shock treatment.*

By 1959 Sidney and Toby Reed were at the end of their joint rope. A decade prior they had moved to Long Island from gritty Brooklyn to enjoy the delights of wholesome, suburban Freeport. Dad was an accountant and Mum was a good-looking typist, as evidenced by the fact that she won a pageant titled Queen of the Stenographers, which sounds an awful lot like a Shangri-Las song.

By the age of seventeen, attention-junkie Lou—a kooky, creative kid who compulsively wrote songs and poetry—was doing everything in his power to torpedo the Utopian fantasies of his parents and challenge the notion of the "nice Jewish boy." When

---

* In fairness to the memory of Lou's parents and in deference to the wishes of Lou's sister, psychotherapist Merrill Weiner, I would like to emphasize that Lou's swishy antics were part of a package and not the sole reason Lou was subjected to this treatment.

he wasn't tormenting his family by extracting earsplitting wails from his electric guitar, he was throwing tantrums and—here comes the most lethal activity of all—he was acting gay, prancing and posing and generally behaving like somebody the neighbors might mistake for one of those terrifying inverts who drown their sorrows at the Hayloft in Freeport, the local gay bar, which, by the way, young Lou was already frequenting.

Freudian ideas dominated American psychiatry back then. Sigmund Freud saw homosexuality as a form of arrested development. (It was a bit like being a rock star.) He did not feel it was possible to "cure" this condition. However, he subscribed to the idea that since—according to Siggy—human beings were essentially bisexual, homosexual impulses could be discouraged, and heterosexual impulses could be nurtured to the point where they might then coexist alongside the gay stuff, allowing, say, the dude in question to marry and have kids. I have several gay peers who, upon revealing their sexual identity to their otherwise free-thinking American parents, were met with a don't-worry-we-can-fix-this-let's-go-see-my-shrink response. Sidney and Toby, like my dad, legitimately feared for their son's survival at a time when homosexuality frequently had catastrophic outcomes.* *Et voilà!* They surrendered their only son, aged seventeen, to a shrink who recommended a course of high-voltage electric shock treatments at Creedmoor Psychiatric Hospital.

----

* This is not to imply that catastrophic outcomes are entirely a thing of the past. We still live in a world where trans women are brutalized and some countries retain the death penalty for homosexuality.

The grim brutality of these sessions—the endless corridors, the locking and unlocking of doors, the restraints, the twitching, the seizures, the spitting, the terror—had a lasting effect on Lou and became part of his legend. The aftermath of each session plunged Lou into a torpid state that resembled senility. "You can't read a book because you get to page 17 and you have to go right back to page 1 again. If you walked around the block, you forgot where you were," Lou reportedly recalled to a friend. Somehow he survived, but with fairly horrifying deficits. According to biographer Victor Bockris, "The shock treatments helped eradicate any feeling of compassion he might have had and handed him a fragmented approach. 'I think everybody has a number of personalities,' he told a friend, to whom he showed a small notebook in which he had written, 'From Lou #3 to Lou #8—Hi!' 'You wake up in the morning and say, "Wonder which of them is around today?" You find out which one and send him out. Fifteen minutes later, someone else shows up. That's why if there's no one left to talk to, I can always listen to a couple of them talking in my head. I can talk to myself.'"

How long did these extreme effects last? His subsequent struggles with addiction and interpersonal meshuggaas suggest that they lingered, but there is no reliable way to separate the electric-shock trauma from the slings and arrows that subsequently came his way.

Did it "fix" the gay thing? Lou's sexuality, the subject of so much speculation during his lifetime, is not easily understood. It's a bit like reading "The Waste Land," the T. S. Eliot poem, which Lou loved. You are enjoying the ride, but you never quite feel that you know what the actual fuck is going on. Lou's love life zigged and zagged, recalling the patterns of courageous self-dramatizing viragos like Vita Sackville-West and Madonna. As you will see,

Lou flows into other people's beds and their lives purely based on the person, rather than the gender. Lou was tortured with electric shocks to eliminate his Liberace and his Paul Lynde, after which he became more of a Marlene Dietrich. His fluidity and his gay solidarity—wildly at odds with midcentury America—align him more with today's youth, who embrace pansexuality and queerness with casual élan.

My dad's gays-are-doomed thesis did not have the desired effect on me, but it certainly got me thinking. I knew that he was largely correct, and that we poofs—and wee poofs like me—were ubiquitously reviled. Homosexuality was still illegal on both sides of the Atlantic. Gay bashing was a local sport in my hometown. Despite a cavalcade of downsides, there was nothing I could really do about my urges. Try as I might to fantasize about sex with Jayne Mansfield, my mind always strayed back to my handsome scoutmaster with the hairy knees. My only option was to adopt a Pollyanna attitude.

There was cause for tentative optimism. I had already clocked the window dressers at the local department store, creating magic in the display windows with their staple guns, scampering up and down ladders in their tight pants and flowery shirts. As far as I could see, they seemed to be having a whale of a time. And Oscar Wilde? Wasn't he the toast of the Mauve Decade, at least for a while? I saw no reason to think of myself as a victim. When people told my mother she was less-than because she was Irish, she pushed back. Betty Doonan always made a point of passing her resilience and her confidence on to me. Me: "The other kids are saying things about me at school." Mum (rhetorically): "They're all ugly so who cares what they think?"

I was a fashion-obsessed teenager coming of age in the Swinging Sixties. The Kinks were my favorite band, and Dusty

Springfield was my everything. Glamour was shimmering on the horizon. I would propel myself toward it and find the groovy people. I would embrace my marginal status and become a fabulous something-or-other. Hold that thought.

I would spend the rest of my teen years aggressively pursuing fabulosity, fashion, and music. In 1967 I am fifteen and already planning my escape to Swinging London—homosexuality between consenting adults finally has been legalized. Yippee. I go to festivals. I worship Jimi Hendrix and see him play at the Isle of Wight Music Festival. (My current dog is called Foxylady.) I attend the first Reading Festival, free concerts in Hyde Park, including, in 1970, the Pink Floyd gathering where a hot dog stand explodes and, if my memory serves me correctly, lightly scalds several hippies. The Velvet Underground, hippie haters that they were, would have taken a sadistic delight in this. But let's not get ahead of ourselves.

By 1970 I am living in Manchester, and post-Jimi, my focus is shifting inexorably to David Bowie. Pictures of Starman adorn the wall of my college hovel. I read an interview in which he bangs on relentlessly about Warhol's band the Velvet Underground. Yes, Andy Warhol, the former fashion illustrator turned pop artist + sculptor + filmmaker + obsessive documentarian + Factory manager + magazine editor + philosopher + social butterfly + cultural icon + eventual mentor to artists such as Jean-Michel Basquiat and Keith Haring, is now the overlord of a happening new band named the Velvet Underground.

So I buy the album with the banana on the cover and start wrapping my head around the whole VU downtown-Manhattan situation.

Manchester University is a serious live music venue. The Who, Led Zeppelin, Jethro Tull, and the rest have all graced us with their presence. In October of '71 it's the turn of the Velvet Underground. I purchase a ticket. 55p.* Chills.

While we wait patiently for the show to begin, Maureen (Moe) Tucker walks onstage carrying a toolbox, extricates a hammer and a nail, and begins pounding her drum kit into the stage. Like a blasé apartment janitor, she takes her sweet time. It is a brilliant piece of rock theatre, and well worth the price of admission. Her message is clear: *I am going to demolish your hearing with my drumming.*

Eventually the guys amble onto the stage—shades, black clothing head to foot, fabulously druggy, doomed, and Warhol-y—grab their instruments, and launch straight into an eardrum-shredding version of "I'm Waiting for the Man." Despite the absence of Nico, my pals and I surrender to the onslaught. We are hypnotized, mesmerized, pasteurized. We are now part of a totally heavy scene, man. We are blown away by John Cale and Lou and Sterling Morrison and Moe! We bray on for weeks about this heavy and meaningful experience to anyone who will listen and give disdainful looks to anyone who was not cool enough to have scored a ticket.

Then we find out the truth.

I stumble upon the appalling tidbit in *New Musical Express*, or maybe it was *Melody Maker*. Turns out that, with the exception of Miss Tucker, we were basically watching a tribute band. John Cale, long gone, had been fired by Lou in 1968. Sterling Morrison

---

* Approximately a dollar. I'm not claiming to remember the price. I Googled the Manchester gig and found stubs that sentimental attendees had thoughtfully archived online.

had returned to college to study something or other. And, most shocking of all, Lou Reed had quit on August 23, 1970—over a year earlier!—and, horror of horrors, is back living with his parents and working in his dad's accounting office.

The substitute lineup was as follows: Moe; Doug Yule; Willie Alexander; and Walter Powers on bass. And I swear they were really good! In the course of researching this book I watched a YouTube interview with Bowie where he admits to having done exactly the same thing. Except he flew to New York and yammered for eons backstage with Doug Yule, thinking it was Lou, and then flew back to the UK, none the wiser. Welcome to life before the internet.

To say I am chagrined about Lou's retreat would be putting it mildly. This news runs counter to my mission of glamorous gay emancipation. It is thoroughly depressing, a bit like finding out that Bowie has thrown in the towel on the whole superstardom thing, gone back to Mum and Dad in Beckenham, and is working as a receptionist in a local failing hair salon. Lou has abandoned his rock dreams and in doing so has cast a deadly pall upon the lives of all the fans who are living vicariously through him. If this sounds a bit melodramatic, then cast your mind back to the drama of your early fan fixations, when everything was either orgasmic or fatal.

Fast-forward one year.

On June 16, 1972, Bowie releases *The Rise and Fall of Ziggy Stardust and the Spiders from Mars*. On August 19 I lace up my cheapo women's Bata navy-blue platform shoes—I saw a Mick Rock photo of Bowie wearing a pair and snagged them—and head, with a group of chums, to the Finsbury Park Rainbow Theatre to see Bowie perform. Roxy Music, by the way, is the opening act. This flawless Ziggy concert—the mimes, the maquillage, and the costumes by Kansai Yamamoto!—is immediately the stuff of legend. Lives are changed forever. This unforgettable soirée—made immortal, thanks to the presence of the late great photographer Mick Rock—becomes the Woodstock of glam rock. This is no exaggeration.

Everything that preceded this concert suddenly seems dusty, overly earnest, and thoroughly déjà vu. Here is the future and it is swanky, theatrical, devastatingly original, and, to quote Noel Coward, "jagged with sophistication." These kinds of tectonic moments occur every once in a while in rock and in the broader culture. One thinks of Nirvana and the '90s, when Kurt and the boys quietly demolished the hard-rocking bombast of bands like Guns N' Roses with their low-key grunge performances. The high-voltage glamazon supermodels of the early '90s each burned holes in every runway, until Kate Moss popped up in Calvin Klein ads, upstaging those heavily maquillaged viragos with her waiflike natural insouciance. Bowie's Rainbow moment is one such leap.

And thanks to Bowie, I find my people. Every groovy guy, gay, and fruit fly in London is there. And so, unbeknownst to me, is Lou Reed. Not given to lavish praise, Lou subsequently describes the concert as "the greatest thing I have ever seen."

As per the UK rock press, Lou Reed is back from the dead. He is in London recording the *other* album that changes my life and the life of every groovy, sentient person on Earth: *Transformer*. Bowie and his guitarist Mick Ronson, the guy whose instrument Bowie now famously fellates onstage, are producing this solo album for thirty-year-old Lou. Bowie is twenty-five. Ronson is twenty-six. Ah! The audacity of youth.

With *Transformer*, Lou will give us the kinky, druggy, subversive pansexual decadence of the Manhattan underground and, more specifically, the Warhol Factory. "If everybody's not a beauty, then nobody is," declared Warhol in *The Philosophy of Andy Warhol*. Inclusivity is the enduring ethos of the Factory, where socialites swap tips with drag queens and intellectuals spar with models, dope fiends, and hustlers. With the album *Transformer*, the edgy malevolence of the New York underground will be leavened with the playful theatricality, humor, and eccentricity of a London that is in the throes of glam rock. The timing is exquisite.

Firstly, it must be acknowledged that rock is, at this particular time, in dire need of an enema, a face-lift, and a new messiah or two. The culture is desperate for what is already being referred to as the "third generation of rock and roll." In his book *Pin-Ups 1972*, seasoned pop-culture vulture and academic Peter Stanfield describes rock's predicament at that moment as follows: "The first-generation were the original rockers: Elvis, Little Richard, Chuck Berry, Buddy Holly, Gene Vincent and Eddie Cochran. The second-generation were those who were directly and immediately inspired by these innovators: the Beatles, Bob Dylan, the Rolling Stones, the Kinks, the Who. But where it was easy to see the break between first and second iterations, the end of the second cycle and the start of the third was less obvious." Who will capture the young audience that no longer relates to the leftovers of second-generation rock? Lou, David Bowie, Marc Bolan, and Iggy Pop are poised to fill the void.

The year 1972 is also pivotal for social change. The counter-culture revolution of the late '60s has loosened up the stays of midcentury respectability. Women's Lib and Gay Lib are on the march. Marginal grassroots movements are gaining traction. Conventional thinking is now widely frowned upon, at least in the media. Notions of sexual liberation, gender equality, androgyny, camp, unisex style, and bisexuality are endlessly dissected. The whole concept of being gay is now a subject for mainstream debate. Cue *Transformer*. Three years later, Lou would reflect on his talents in a taped conversation with a friend in Rotterdam, which could speak to the critical timing of the album, as follows: "I am not original. . . . My timing was perfect."

Creative types find themselves drawn to the transgressive aspect of gayness. Even confirmed hets like Rod Stewart are frosting their tips and vamping in pink satin suits.* In a 1998 doc titled *Lou Reed: Rock and Roll Heart*, Lou recalls his '72 *Transformer* moment as follows: "Glam rock, androgyny, polymorphic sex—I was right in the middle of it. Some say I could have been at the head of the class." This is the aspect of *Transformer* that casts its spell over me. Stylish and modish and gay-positive, this album is the soundtrack for the new shiny, draggy, tarty, silver-snakeskin, electric-blue satin fabulosity that is central to my world.

The success of *Transformer* is, therefore, almost overdetermined. Not only does it sound fresh and relevant—the possible beginnings of the third generation of rock, as described by Peter Stanfield—but also it is the perfect soundtrack for the new glamdrogyny. (Sorry. Could not resist this nounportunity.)

Transformer soars and becomes the most enduring and popular part of Lou's legacy. Half a century later *Transformer* will not be silenced. This album reflects a moment when Lou, enabled by those outrageous Brits, took a look at the Warhol milieu and

---

* Hets: a very British abbreviation from the time period in question. I won't insult the reader by spelling it out.

elected to pay homage with a gay album. It is beautiful and poetic, and yes, it is ultra camp. C-A-M-P. This is why it means so much to any kid who'd ever minced round their backyard, observed by parents with furrowed brows. As the late great Philip Core, erotic artist and writer, once said, camp is "the lie that tells the truth."

This album sounds just as fresh today as it did when Holly Woodlawn and Candy Darling and Jackie Curtis—these Warhol superstar drag queens are key players in the saga of *Transformer*—were hanging out at Max's Kansas City, their favorite New York dive. Why is that?

For starters, please note that there is no moral posturing in Lou's lyrics. No self-pity, no mawkish sentimentality, and no fake optimism. The tales of Candy, Holly, and Jackie just *are*. This is life. Pathos and beauty and pain. It's like a Diane Arbus photograph. Deal with it. *Transformer* has a unique vibe because it marries the street realism of Reed's gritty side with the perfume and sophistication of camp. This combo is at the heart of its originality and enduring fascination.

Lou Reed gave us much to be grateful for. With the Velvet Underground he brought sadomasochism, literacy, and perversity to the rock world. He and John Cale and Nico made it de rigueur not to smile when somebody takes your picture. They created the first alliance between pop music and the avant-garde. Both with the VU and subsequently as a solo artist, Lou made great art for us, and in the process he suffered. He made others suffer too in all manner of cringeworthy ways.

His greatest and most enduring gift will be *Transformer* and, of course, the final track on side 1, "Walk on the Wild Side." With this album, he offered us—the glorious smorgasbord of LGBTQ+—freedom from the compulsion to seek the approval of others. We inverts had already wasted far too much time hoping and praying that the world might one day bless and anoint our flowery fabulosity, our naughty proclivities, our flamboyant foulards, our love of camp, our histrionic hully gullies, our purple ostrich feathers, satins, and velvets, and our frothy, subversive worldview. Lou offered liberation from the need to meet corny conventional expectations. He gave us a soundtrack for our lives that is bold and brave and dazzling. *Transformer* is an album that celebrates, humanizes, romanticizes, ennobles, and immortalizes the drag queens, the super-freaks, and the misfits of the world.

Happy fiftieth anniversary, Lou, wherever the fuck you are.

Legendary activist Marsha P. Johnson in 1970 outside Bellevue
Hospital, protesting their use of shock treatments, drugs, and
imprisonment on gay people.

(Diana Davies, New York Public Library archive)

CHAPTER 1

We're Coming Out

Brigitte Bardot's lips begat Mick Jagger's lips. According to fashion icon Diana Vreeland, Bardot's bouche "prepared the way for the sixties and made the sixties alluring rather than just ugly. Her lips made Mick Jagger's lips possible." What was DV's point? To embrace and understand new styles and cultural moments, we, the general public, might need a little warm-up, a little marination, a little preparation. Mick Jagger's jolie-laide beauty was embraced and worshipped because we, the audience, had already spent years being prepped by Bardot's magnificent pout.

So, if that is the case, what made *Transformer* possible?

Transformer is like a giant gold and black piñata. When it was released in 1972, we each grabbed a stick and started shrieking and swinging. Out poured kink, poetry, glamour, trash, drag queens, hustlers, dope, genius, originality, and—drumroll—validation, confirmation, and encouragement for a broad swath of young people who were figuring out how to be themselves.

To understand how *Transformer* became such a significant cultural monument, we are well served to examine the decade prior. The warm-up. Now, as an old queen with time on my hands and a desire to share, I raise my lorgnette to my wrinkled visage and look back at this period, assuming the role of guide.

The run-up to *Transformer* was a period of bonkers contrasts. For example: appalling images from the wars in the Congo and Vietnam alternated idiotically with shots of dolly birds wearing frocks by Mary Quant and white boots by André Courrèges. News of assassinations and terrorist bombings were interspersed with have-a-nice-day TV commercials selling mayonnaise and Tussy deodorant.

The biggest contrasts were generational. Typical '60s teens looked nothing like their parents. Plonk my sister and my mother next to each other and you were looking at two different species. My sister, Shelagh, the bird-watching back-to-nature girl with beatnik leanings, grooved on Buffy Sainte-Marie and Joan Baez. My mother, with her overpainted lips and upswept hairdo, aspired to the immaculate glamour of a 1940s film-noir heroine. Things came to a head when Sheel began to ovulate. My mother marked the occasion by presenting her with a girdle, a rite of passage for the women of her generation. My sister flung it back at her. During the decade prior to *Transformer*, mothers and daughters all over the Western Hemisphere were flinging foundation garments back and forth. Compare with today's mothers and daughters, who text each other constantly, gleefully share clothes, and—thanks to hair extensions and Botox—appear identical.

And then there was the gay stuff. World War II had been won. The Nazis had been vanquished. New bogeymen were needed. Commies and pansies filled the void. In his book *The Velvet Mafia: The Gay Men Who Ran the Swinging Sixties*, Darryl W. Bullock describes the moment as follows: "With Nazism crushed, homosexuality and the threat of 'Reds under the bed' became the joint anathema of the British press." The same applies in the US, where a moral panic, which came to be known as the Lavender Scare, took root, spearheaded by Joseph McCarthy and Roy Cohn. Paranoid obsessions with both the commies and the gays dominated culture in a way that now seems almost cultlike.

For a more granular assessment of the pre-*Transformer* period, I want to get chronological on your ass.

In 1962 the Everly Brothers have a huge hit with "Crying in the Rain." The close harmonies of these two handsome brothers make me shiver, and I spend far too much time attempting to figure out which bro—Phil or Don—will be my boyfriend. On a semi-related note, Illinois becomes the first state to remove the sodomy law from criminal code. It took a while to get there. In the eighteenth century buggery laws inherited from the Brits awarded homosexuals with the death penalty. Though the laws were rarely enforced, the tacit threat must surely have put a damper on many a campfire cuddle. In the early nineteenth century US law pre-scribed massive fines and copious lashes, and I don't mean the thick, silky kind favored by top-notch drag queens.

On December 17, 1963, the *New York Times* runs a front-page story with the headline "Growth of Overt Homosexuality in the City Provokes Wide Concern." This sad article depicts a twilight world of "deviates" frequenting establishments called, for exam-ple, the Fawn and the Heights Supper Club. It contains many sentences that would elicit a guffaw from a contemporary reader. Example: "Inverts are to be found in every conceivable line of work from trucking to coupon clipping." The piece also refers to "a homophile movement" that is agitating for change. At right about this time a twenty-one-year-old Lou Reed starts to agitate his parents by practicing his new gay walk, also provoking wide concern. The first gay demonstration in the US takes place on September 19 of that year at the Whitehall Street Induction Cen-ter in NYC, protesting against discrimination in the military. In an era when so many people are thinking of ways to avoid the army it is shocking to contemplate the fact that there are worthy gays trying to claw their way in and die for their country. This speaks to the strength of the desire for equality, and/or the impulse to escape poverty.

On November 22 of that year Kennedy is assassinated, and Warhol, a year into his silk-screening technique, immediately makes art out of the tragedy. He grabs the newspaper images and transposes them into cool, detached portraits of widow Jackie in a way that memorializes the media rather than the tragedy. As per communication theorist Marshall McLuhan, "The medium is the message." Lou Reed later writes his own finely crafted homage to JFK—"The Day John Kennedy Died"—including it on his 1982 album *The Blue Mask*.

In 1964 the Beatles famously occupy the top five positions on *Billboard* charts. A new cultural revolution is underway. On the more esoteric front, this is also the year that Warhol's pal Susan Sontag, writing in the *Partisan Review*, unleashes her "Notes on 'Camp,'" effectively demolishing the distinction between high and low culture.

Before we digress into the world of camp, we need to pause and answer a simple question: Where are all the lesbians? The story of *Transformer* is dripping with gay men, but not exactly drenched with their female counterparts. Most lesbians—my sister, Shelagh, is a great example—eschewed the fashionable exhibitionistic professions that tantalized gay men in favor of more meaningful vocations, such as social work, teaching, activism, and, in Susan Sontag's case, academia.

Sontag, like many lesbians of her generation, chose to keep her sexual identity on the down-low for most of her life. In 2005 she gave an interview to *Out* magazine in which she, with her usual brutal candor, clarified her stance, and that of many others: "I grew up in a time when the modus operandi was the 'open secret.' I'm used to that, and quite OK with it. Intellectually, I know why I haven't spoken more about my sexuality, but I do wonder if I haven't repressed something there to my detriment. Maybe I could have given comfort to some people if I had dealt with the subject of my private sexuality more, but it's never been my prime mission to give comfort, unless somebody's in drastic need. I'd rather give pleasure, or shake things up."

Back to 1964.

"Notes on 'Camp'" is Sontag's academic attempt to spotlight true camp and differentiate it from that which is merely tacky or kitsch, or ironic. (Tellingly, an early version was titled "Notes on Homosexuality.") Since the concept of camp is central to the controversies that swirled around Lou Reed and *Transformer*, it seems important to attempt to explain Sontag's attempt to explain this hard-to-explain concept.

Camp for Sontag is an exercise in failed seriousness. She highlights camp's trash-loving, it's-good-because-it's-awful aesthetic. She also addresses camp's demented enthusiasm, describing it as follows: "Camp sees everything in quotation marks. It's not a lamp, but a 'lamp'; not a woman, but a 'woman.'"

It is no exaggeration to say that Sontag's "Notes" ignites a shit-storm. The establishment goes into meltdown. The old order, which prizes good taste and refinement, suddenly realizes their world is under threat. Sontag's decadent attempts to elevate vulgarity are plainly unacceptable. This androgynous upstart with her camp utterances is clearly intent upon stealing the entire culture out from under their noses and absconding with it, and then divvying it up amongst her disgusting Greenwich Village friends—smelly bohemians, denizens of Andy Warhol's Factory, and sundry intellectuals. How dare she equate tacky stuff with highbrow art? How can she put *Swan Lake* in the same category as singer La Lupe and Flash Gordon comics? How can she suggest there is anything positive about bad taste?

In the ensuing brouhaha, Sontag is featured in various national publications, including the *New York Times Magazine*. A subsequent letter of complaint from a Mrs. Roberta Copeland of Philly includes the following warning: "if the concept of Camp is to be allowed to enter the mainstream of our cultural life, with the blessing, no less, of the *New York Times*, then I think our society is headed for a moral collapse unlike anything we've ever seen." To which all the Factory gays doubtless shriek, "How camp! Can't wait!"

Overnight the conventional notions of art become vulnerable to this radical new way of thinking: the old-school curators and academics are terrified that this rising generation of young reprobates are poised to steal all the goodies. Their fears of a camp coup d'état prove justified. It doesn't happen overnight. By the time *Transformer* is released, eight years later, all the trendiest people are collecting art-nouveau vases and Warhol Brillo boxes and soup cans, and irony and postmodernism are at the center of culture.

Sontag was an edgy, high-brow bluestocking. As a result, "Notes on 'Camp,'" though visionary, is a tad confusing. I have my own simplified definition that coexists with Sontag's but makes camp a little easier to understand and apply. Here goes: In my opinion, camp is simply a matter of doing things *as if* you are doing them. Diving into a swimming pool? Throw your arms heavenward and give it the full Esther Williams treatment. When you dive into a pool *as if* you are diving into a pool, as opposed to executing an earnest quotidian plop, the result is magical—that pool is transformed from a grody Band Aid–strewn chlorine bath into a veritable *LAGOON*! Smoking a cigarette? Perform the action *as if* you are a French existentialist. My *as if* theory applies to all actions, great and small. Want to be a rock star? Then present yourself *as if* you are a rock star. We will see how this plays out for Lou a decade later.

Back to 1964. This is also the year that Lou Reed graduates from the Syracuse University with a BA in English and concentrates his energies on evading the draft.

March 1965: The Selma to Montgomery March becomes Bloody Sunday, and the brutal images define the Civil Rights Movement. The Voting Rights Act of 1965, signed into law by President Lyndon B. Johnson on August 6, aims to remove the legal barriers at the state and local levels that prevent African Americans from exercising their right to vote as per the Fifteenth Amendment to the US Constitution. The VRA is lauded as one of the most far-reaching pieces of civil rights legislation in US history. Activists in the LGBTQ+ community are encouraged, invigorated, and inspired.

Meanwhile, down on the Lower East Side, the formation of the Velvet Underground is underway. John Cale, a classically trained musician from Wales with the look of a gorgeous degenerate Rasputin, and Lou Reed have found each other and are ensconced at 56 Ludlow Street, within pickle-tossing distance of Katz's Deli. Jack Smith, the legendary avant-garde trans filmmaker and moldy-glam icon, whose film *Flaming Creatures* opened two years prior, is their neighbor. In November, Cale's pal, musician Tony Conrad, finds in the gutter a paperback about suburban kink titled *The Velvet Underground* and takes it to Ludlow Street. The Warlocks, previously the Primitives, now have their true name.

Victor Bockris's description of their bohemian lifestyle calls to mind the residential splendor enjoyed by Ratso Rizzo and Joe

Buck in the movie *Midnight Cowboy*: "There was no heat or hot water, and the landlord collected the rent with a gun. When it got cold during February to March of 1965, they ran into the streets, grabbed some wooden crates, and threw them into the fireplace, or often sat hunched over their instruments with carpets wrapped around their shoulders. When the toilet stopped up, they picked up the shit and threw it out the window. For sustenance they cooked big pots of porridge or made vegetable pancakes, eating the same glop day in and day out as if it were fuel." Safe to say there was no Shake Shack on Astor Place back then.

Despite the hardships, or maybe because of them, Lou feels something has clicked, recalling, "We heard our screams turn into songs and then back into screams again." The marriage of Lou's poetry and Cale's avant-garde approach produces gold.

In 1966 the Compton's Cafeteria Riot breaks out in a San Francisco eatery after trans women and drag queens are denied service for "breaking gendered clothing laws." The rioters are habitués of the Tenderloin area, girls who, like Holly and Jackie and Candy, were forced to Walk on the Wild Side by a hostile society. "A lot of people thought we were sick, mental trash," recalled participant Felicia "Flames" in 2014 to blogger Monika Kowalska, adding, "Nobody cared whether we lived or died. Our own families abandoned us and we had nowhere to go."

In NYC, Andy Warhol makes an announcement: "We're sponsoring a new band. It's called the Velvet Underground . . . We have this chance to combine music and art and films . . . and if it works out, it might be very glamorous." Commencing in April 1966, Andy stages the Exploding Plastic Inevitable, a multisensory multimedia series of happenings at the Dom on Saint Mark's Place, showcasing his new pet project the Velvet Underground. The lineup consists of Lou; Cale; Sterling Morrison, a guitarist Lou met through a college friend; and androgynous and self-taught Maureen Tucker on drums. Nico, an otherworldly monosyllabic ice-blond German ex-model in a white suit, is now their lead singer. In her book *Glittering Images*, Camille Paglia, yet another brilliant lesbian academic and thinker, describes Warhol's EPI as follows: "Shifting into music and performance art, . . . he created a psychedelic environment for them at the Dom, a Lower East Side hall where strobe lights and a mirror ball (which he found in a junk shop) forged the template for future discotheques."

Across the pond, the sun comes out from behind a cloud: in 1967 the Sexual Offences Act legalizes homosexual acts between consenting adults over the age of twenty-one. My memory of this moment—I was fifteen years old—is inextricably tied to an anti-gay article that appeared around this time in the *News of the World*, England's most salacious tabloid. The writer ventured into the wilds of Hampstead Heath in North London and interviewed cruising homosexuals. According to the scribe, the tart-tongued gays he encountered were attired in white turtleneck sweaters (all of them) and spent their evenings draped on the branches of various trees on the lookout for "trade." This kind of reporting is intended to send shivers of revulsion down the spine. Needless to say, it does not have the desired effect on me. The description of this alternative gay utopia enthralls me. Hampstead Heath seems like a safari park for chicly attired inverts. And if it starts raining you can head home—in your matching sweaters—and enjoy a consenting shag, because now it's legal.

One year later the sun disappears. Martin Luther King Jr. is assassinated in April 1968. A few months later Senator Bobby Kennedy meets the same fate. Sadness and darkness. In June Valerie Solanas, a fanatical feminist who is the author of the S.C.U.M.

Manifesto—S.C.U.M. = the Society for Cutting Up Men—enters the Factory and attempts to assassinate Andy Warhol by riddling his body with bullets. Lou responds by inking up his quill and writing a haunting song titled "Andy's Chest," which, three years later, will get the Bowie-Ronson treatment on *Transformer*.

In 1969 the world gets sexier. Serge Gainsbourg, France's most famous songwriter, and his style-icon girlfriend Jane Birkin—the Hermès "Birkin" bag was named in homage to her—enjoy massive success with their orgasmic heavy-breathing duet "Je t'aime . . . moi non plus." Despite being a number one hit in the UK, "Je t'aime" is banned by the BBC and various US radio stations. Fortunately for moi, my sister, Sheel, has a copy, so we are able to enjoy the delights of Miss Birkin's over-the-top climax. It is a great example of camp. Deadly serious, and therefore ultimately hilarious.

This year also gives us the Manson murders, Woodstock, and, most important, Stonewall, the defining moment of twentieth-century LGBTQ+ history. I won't insult the reader with a blow-by-blow presentation of all the facts. Suffice it to say, this is the night when a diverse group of courageous individuals, carousing at a neighborhood bar on Christopher Street, throws down the velvet gauntlet, takes to the barricades, and declares war on police harassment.

Soixante-neuf is big for me. It is the year I become spellbound by Andy Warhol. My fascination is triggered by a school trip to see Warhol's iconic exhibit at the Tate Gallery in London. I drool over photographs of Jane Forth, Joe Dallesandro, and Andy Warhol. Why? It's the not-smiling thing again. I find their unsmilingness weirdly validating. It makes me happy. The whole world seems to use smiling to gloss over the brutality and horror of life. Excessive smiling is like an act of appeasement. Lou Reed's commitment to not smiling is a fuck-you to the prevailing have-a-nice-day cheeriness and an acknowledgment that there is often not much to smile about. Lou, like Victoria Beckham, will go down in history as one of the greatest non-smilers.

The Cockettes, a group of hippies and drag queens who live in a San Francisco commune named Kaliflower, fly cross-country and perform in New York; the shambolic evening propels a number of New Yorkers toward the exits, including Andy Warhol and Gore Vidal. There emerges an East Coast/West Coast rivalry, an augur of the Biggie vs. Tupac East Coast/West Coast rapper war of the late twentieth century. Every member of the VU has confessed to a loathing for hippies, especially when in LA. As per John Cale: "Our attitude to the West Coast is one of hate and derision." The West Coasters are less than receptive to the East Coast vibes. Bockris describes a typical reaction as follows: "Flouncing out of the club on the first night, a terrified Cher snapped that the music would replace nothing except, perhaps, suicide (a quote the Warhol people could not but relish)."

The first "Gay Liberation Day March" is held in NYC in 1970. This is also the year that Marsha P. Johnson and Sylvia Rivera co-found Street Transvestites Action Revolutionaries (STAR). Sylvia and Marsha are anti-assimilationists, a brave stance for which they both pay a biblical price.

Jimi Hendrix plays at the Isle of Wight Festival in August 1970. As previously mentioned, I am present. Yes, it is magical. Less fabulous? He dies a few weeks later, joining Jim and Janis and MLK and JFK and Sharon Tate and so many others. Grab the black crepe, *again!* Between Vietnam and drugs and assassinations, the early 1960s into the early 1970s is a decade of death. Who's next?

On a more cheery note: in 1971 Holly, Jackie, and Candy go mainstream, sort of, with *Women in Revolt.* The trio previously appeared in various Andy Warhol–Paul Morrissey movies, but this new scorcher is the most amusing, the most entertaining, and, as a result, plays regularly in arty independent movie houses. The joy of watching trans women taking on the roles of earnest and irate feminists never loses its punch. One wonders if this satire might have been Paul and Andy's way of getting back at the extremes of radical feminism—as exemplified by trigger-happy extremist Valerie Solanas and her S.C.U.M. Manifesto, which had almost cost Warhol his life.

The year 1972. Now, here's something the Vikings could never have predicted: Sweden becomes the first country to make transgender surgery legal and supported. In an equally progressive move, San Francisco strikes down employment discrimination based on sexual orientation. On July 1 a "carnival parade" of protest is held in London from Hyde Park to Trafalgar Square. It is the first Gay Pride March in the UK and the nearest Saturday to the Stonewall uprising date of June 28. I recall this first Gay Pride March as a street-theatre-ish moment. There are tap dancers, and mimes in whiteface. It is important to remember that mimes go largely unmocked at this time. It all seems fresh and new, especially in the context of youth culture. Bowie regularly incorporates mime moves—man-trapped-in-a-box!—into his act with great success. Speaking of whom: one month later Lou and Bowie and Ronson concoct *Transformer* at Trident Studios in nearby Soho. The album is released on November 8.

The velocity of change during the ten-year run-up to *Transformer*'s creation is unprecedented. We go from black and white to psychedelia, from speed to smack, from ardent homophobia to casual homophobia and intermittent acceptance, from winkle pickers to space boots, from the Supremes to Labelle, from Liberace to Wayne County (eventually Jayne County), from Judy to Liza, from bouffants to mullets and shags, from JFK to Richard

Nixon, from sweater sets to unisex, from Yuri Gagarin to "Space Oddity," from Slinkys to *Deep Throat*. Sex clubs, massage parlors, and leather bars proliferate. If it feels good, people are doing it. And if it feels bad, people are doing it even more.

And when being naughty lost its sizzle you could always turn on the box. During this period the entire population switches from radio to TV. The horrors and the injustices and the cleansing cream ads and the bombings and the touchdowns and the game-show shrieking and the Maxwell House gurgling and the soaps and the szhoosh are blasted into the brains of the population on a daily basis. And, if the lyrics to "Satellite of Love" are any indication, Lou is watching it all.

Early dawning: Paul Morrissey, Andy Warhol, and Lou Reed on the Velvet
Underground's 1966 tour bus in Michigan.

(Nat Finkelstein Estate)

CHAPTER 2

LOU

In 1975, three years after the launch of *Transformer*, Lou Reed is talking to a friend in Rotterdam when someone switches on a tape recorder, and that recording ends up nearly a half century later in the New York Public Library special holdings. It's a casual, freewheeling conversation during which he makes an oh-my-god-did-he-just-say-that statement about the primary intention of this album: "I thought it was dreary for gay people to have to listen to straight people's love songs. So we did this. This is a large corporation putting this out with a lot of money."

Here was a revolutionary declaration, unprecedented and bold, made at a time when many thought gay people were not entitled to any kind of songs, never mind love songs. How did Lou, the guy who allegedly lost his empathy during all that gruesome electric shock treatment, become this empathetic artist, a guy who would calmly embark on such a politically and socially risky, commercially unviable project? What is his story?

Early Lou is dark. Biographer Victor Bockris describes him as follows: "Like a shark, he had an urge to poke at dead bodies until he found a live one, then devour it as ferociously as he could, letting the blood run down his chin." *And Victor is a huge fan.* Imagine what Lou's detractors say about him.

The truth is young Lou is hard to love. Much of his behavior—drugs, smashing his hand through a window, doling out verbal and physical abuse—is cringeworthy and incomprehensible.

But Lou owns his darkness, describing his college self as "a rather negative, strung-out, violent, aggressive person." A Dionysian side rages throughout his early life. But there is also an Apollonian side. He believes in art, flinging himself, according to Victor Bockris, into music appreciation, opera, literature, and philosophy. He later tells Bockris, "I was very into Hegel, Sartre, Kierkegaard." After reading the latter, he describes his passionate reaction as follows: "You feel like something horrible has happened to you—fear and nothing. That's where I was coming from."

In addition to being dark, or quite possibly because of it, Lou is also relentlessly driven to create. Reading about the fecundity of his college years—forming bands, spewing poems, reading Baudelaire, precociously writing songs, including "I'm Waiting for the Man" and "Heroin," chasing down eccentric mentors like the legendary Delmore Schwartz,* penning short stories—is a dizzying and shame-making experience that leaves one wanting to hop into a time machine and revise one's own less than productive collegiate experience.

Like Dylan, Hendrix, or Joni Mitchell; Brian Jones, Pete Townshend, or Lennon-McCartney, Lou is one of those '60s in-

----

* Delmore Schwartz, poet and short-story writer, head case and alcoholic, taught Lou at Syracuse and massively influenced his approach to writing. All that dour, surreal, incomprehensible stuff that sounds so great when set to crashing guitars comes from Schwartz. Throughout his life Lou cited Schwartz and Warhol as his biggest influences.

dividuals whose desire to express themselves in a poetic, original manner via music is uncontainable. Lou learns to play the guitar from listening to the radio. His instrument of choice is the 1964 Gretsch 6122 Country Gentleman. Within a very short period of time, while still in college, he finds collaborators and puts together a band, LA and the Eldorados. They play frat parties, clubs, and bars, two or three nights a week, driving to gigs in a '59 Chrysler with massive fins and making $125 per gig.

After graduating in '64 he takes an in-house job at a music publishing company with the oddly Dickensian name of Pickwick International, churning out rip-off pop songs to go, some of which actually get recorded. Lou pens a hilarious dance "hit" titled "The Ostrich." The absurdist lyrics exhort dancers to stomp on each other's heads, a harbinger of the fantasy violence advocated in several Reed compositions, including the *Transformer* song "Vicious." Sensing they might have a potential hit on their hands, Pickwick decides to cobble together a fake band, the Primitives, and take "The Ostrich" on the road, promoting this catchy idiocy at high school dances. Lou Reed and John Cale meet serendipitously when they are dragooned into the Primitives. So begins one of the noteworthiest collaborations in the history of rock.

During long hours in their shared Ludlow Street hovel, Lou and Cale develop what will become the legendary droning, twanging, thumping sound of the Velvet Underground. Cale is dripping with avant-garde cred. This classically trained musician, a Welshman, is a former collaborator with John Cage—they participated in the first ever eighteen-hour forty-minute marathon recital of an Erik Satie piece titled "Vexations"—and a member of La Monte Young's Theatre of Eternal Music. He and his electric viola are tuned in to the musical potential of every-thing around him, including the hum of the refrigerator.

From 1965 to 1970 Lou and Cale and Sterling Morrison and Maureen Tucker create the grooviest, coolest band in history. Yes, there's Pink Floyd and Cream and Sly and the Family Stone and Led Zeppelin, but the Velvet Underground are somehow floating above—a bit like one of Andy Warhol's helium-filled Mylar pillows from the Exploding Plastic Inevitable—in their own category of avant-garde, esoteric cool. What makes the Velvet Underground so terminally and eternally legendary? So many reasons. Let's start with the superficial fluffy stuff and work our way gradually toward the nitty-gritty profundities.

> **VELVET STYLE:** While other bands of the era still wear nifty matching suits and execute perky choreography, the Velvet Underground are dressed in black clothing and pimp shades and, as previously noted, they never smile, exuding a negative critical energy that, in tandem with the music, puts the audience into a state of hypnotized submission. In this regard, and many others, the VU pave the way for punk, Bauhaus, and Joy Division. When Warhol adds the ice-blond mystery of former-model Nico, you have an assemblage worthy of a photo by Richard Avedon.

The Velvet Underground have a strong connection with fash-ion right from the beginning. After all, what the hell shall the young girl wear to all tomorrow's parties? It's a legitimate ques-tion. This is an era of paper, plastic, and light-up dresses and unisex clothing. Betsey Johnson is the designer for Parapher-nalia, a futuristic emporium located on Madison at 65th Street, which becomes the boutique of choice for the VU after they play the opening party. Betsey goes on a few dates with Sterling Morrison, then switches to John Cale and marries him.

Warhol, Nico, Sterling, Lou, Moe, and various members of the Factory gang, including the legendary Viva "superstar," attend the civic wedding ceremony, Polaroiding wildly. When the city hall judge refuses on principle to marry "a lady in pants," Betsey runs to the ladies' room to strip off the trousers of her burgundy crushed-velvet pantsuit. After adjusting her tights and yanking her jacket down as far as it will go, Betsey defiantly rejoins the delighted wedding party in front of the fuming official. She remains philosophical about this moment: "Remember, in 1967 most women still dressed with a 1950s mindset and wouldn't go out without their gloves matching their purses."

Naturally Betsey makes clothes for her new husband. Cale is a striking, haunted-looking dude. With his pin-straight pageboy coiffure, black turtlenecks, and elaborate society-lady chokers, he appears like a courtier from the Eisenstein movie *Ivan the Terrible*. In the annals of rock style, his accessory choices are singular and extraordinary. Recalls Betsey, "Since John was a poet, after all, I designed clothes for him to look the part. There's something very intimate about making a garment for someone you're really into. I made him these black canvas suits that were perfect for his build and some fancy shirts with ruffles. They were gorgeous and fit perfectly with my fantasy of John." As a further marker of their intimacy, Betsey raids Cale's collection of striped rugby shirts and fashions them into cheeky outfits for herself.

Betsey also designs for Sterling, Moe, and, of course, Lou. Regarding Lou, she remembers, "all *he* ever wanted was a motorcycle jacket and gray suede trousers. His only suggestion was to cut the pants very, very tight through the crotch. He always said that I cut good crotch."

THE SMACK: The Velvet Underground glorify hard drugs, and this, unfortunately for them, is not a pose. Their proximity to dope gives them a frisson of danger. They are genuine outlaws. As Nico famously put it to writer Nick Kent, "I was a hausfrau from Hanover until I discovered heroin."

THE PATRONAGE: The VU are groovy because they have the ultimate blessing—they are Andy Warhol's band. Pop art meets art pop. To showcase his new protégés, Warhol stages, as previously mentioned, the Exploding Plastic Inevitable, a series of live events in various venues, which becomes the ne plus ultra, the Woodstock, of artsy '60s happenings. *Variety* calls it "a three-ring psychosis." Betsey Johnson remembers it well: "Andy's movies were being projected on the walls, the ceiling, and even the crowd, so I was walking through *My Hustler* and *Poor Little Rich Girl* as I tried to make my way closer to the stage. When Nico and the band started in with 'Femme Fatale,' at a deafening volume, the most amazing light show started. . . . I could catch a glimpse now and then of Gerard Malanga and Mary Woronov doing their infamous whip dance—living out their S & M fantasies right onstage! Edie Sedgwick, oblivious to the whip, go-go danced alongside them."

REGARDING GERARD MALANGA AND THAT WHIP DANCE: Malanga was a key Warhol collaborator from '63 to '70. In his memoir of the Velvet Underground, he describes his style of Terpsichore as "a cross between the Frug and an Egyptian belly dance." His first partner was doomed socialite Edie Sedgwick. When Edie drifted from the Factory milieu, she was replaced by statuesque beauty Mary Woronov. In addition to Frugging with Mary, Malanga was responsible for the overall choreography of the Exploding Plastic Inevitable. The whip dance fit perfectly with Lou's celebrations of kink.

THE COUNTER-COUNTERCULTURE. Every aspect of the Velvet Underground is a savage antidote to the emerging culture of peace, love, and flower power. They are self-declared hippie haters, hence the dotted line to punk, a decade later.

THE SOUND. The Velvet Underground sound is not like anything else. Cale's humming and droning electric viola, Reed's pre-punk guitar, Morrison's hypnotic guitar syncopations, Tucker's pile-driving drumming create an alarming and ominous effect. And let's give a massive shout-out to Nico's dirge-like vocals. Her robotic, German-accented singing style, paving the way for Kraftwerk, combines with her unattainable haughty fashion-model glamour—another fuck-you to the audience—to provide a thrilling focal point. She is a singing, unsmiling totem of fascination. Morrissey and Warhol, palpitating over Nico's beauty and style, somehow manage to persuade a reluctant Lou to allow Nico to occupy center stage.

THE CACOPHONY. The Velvets use extended distortion—for reference, listen to the long version of "Sister Ray"—with the deliberate intention of challenging the audience. During the tour of the Exploding Plastic Inevitable, Andy, according to his own recollections, said, "'If they can take it for ten minutes, then we play it for fifteen.' . . . That's our policy. Always leave them wanting less."

And now we come to the pièce de résistance, the Shakespeare of art rock, Mr. Lou Reed, the man Patti Smith would later describe in *The New Yorker* as "our generation's New York poet, championing its misfits as Whitman had championed its workingman and Lorca its persecuted." Yes, the Velvet Underground has style and intelligence, but most important, they have Lou, the bloke Danny Fields, half a century later, still refers to as "the greatest songwriter of his age."*

LOU'S LYRICS: Lou is right up there with Dylan and Joni, minus the folksy stuff. His songs are brutal and beautiful, and they have no moral message. There is no "Poor me," and there is certainly no saccharine and no "Have a nice day." They are the opposite of country songs. They are as bleak as Beckett. And they—"Femme Fatale," "Heroin," "I'm Waiting for the Man," "Sunday Morning"—are as evocative as fuck. Whether writing about agonizing drug withdrawals or aristocratic spanking sessions, Lou serves up realness; he takes you there, always and forever, over and over again, leaving you wanting more (not less).

---

* Danny is one of the great connectors of the music world. He helped launch the Doors, hung out with Warhol, and managed the Ramones. *The Guardian* newspaper calls him "the coolest guy you've never heard of." He graciously agreed to be interviewed for this book.

LOU'S VOCALS: Lou Reed's delivery is uniquely throwaway and deadpan, like a junkie coming out of, or maybe sinking into, a stupor. His brilliance comes from an instinctive and authentic nonchalance. He is very good at sounding amateurish. This is very Warholian. Andy stated in his book of his philosophy, "I can only understand really amateur performers or really bad performers, because whatever they do never really comes off, so therefore it can't be phoney." Lou's instantly recognizable vocals are refreshingly unpolished, sometimes pretentious, but never phoney (Andy's spelling).

LOU'S KINK: Lou digs the Marquis de Sade. He is also inspired by Leopold von Sacher-Masoch and writes "Venus in Furs"—one of the Velvets' most brilliant and strange offerings—as an homage to the 1870 novel of the same name. The VU stage act is all about leather and dominance and submission. The whip dance fits right in. The Velvet Underground are kinky at a time when music audiences barely understand the word. In his essay "'Venus in Furs' by the Velvet Underground," Erich Kuersten writes: "There is no intro or buildup to the song; the track starts as if you opened a door to a decadent Marrakesh S&M/opium den, a blast of air-conditioned Middle Eastern menace with a plodding beat that's the missing link between 'Bolero' and Led Zeppelin's version of 'When the Levee Breaks.'" That about sums it up.

LOU'S CUTENESS: When I interview fashion and culture writer Tim Blanks, he recalls Lou's sexual charisma as follows: "To me he was the most gorgeous creature, with the leather jacket and the shades. Bowie changed my life and my fandom lingers with me now, but I never found him sexy like Lou . . . all those rumors about him having a twelve-inch dick!"

So, back to the original question: How did Lou become the guy who decided to fill the LGBTQ+ void and skew an entire album toward me and my cohort? Writing in 1980, Lester Bangs, one of Lou's most antagonistic detractors, explained why he had idolized early Lou: "Because the things he wrote and sang and played in the Velvet Underground were for me part of the beginning of a real revolution in the whole scheme between men and women, men and men, women and women, humans and humans. And I don't mean clones. I mean a diversity that extends to the stars."*

Given all of the above, given the unconventional nature of Lou's oeuvre, his strange gifts, his personal journey, his pansexual propensities, and his thirst for relentless experimentation—a diversity that extends to the stars—it is not surprising at all that he made the radical decision to give the gays the songs that nobody else was giving them. It was, to use the Yiddish word, *beshert*, the literal translation of which is "meant to be" or "destiny."

Success in the music business is elusive. It's not enough to be an empathetic visionary, or the greatest songwriter of your age.

––––––––

* The term "clones" was used to refer to the hordes of identical mustachioed men who began to fill big-city gay enclaves at this time. In their aviators, plaid shirts, and faded, crotch-mangling Levi's, the "macho" lookalike clones were viewed by us nonclones as sexually audacious, but a tad conformist.

It takes gobs of good luck and extraordinary resilience. In addition you need to be able to juggle the bowel-curdling madness of band membership while simultaneously navigating the financial and legal minefields of the music business, especially when your songs are called "Heroin" and include all that kinky stuff. The sloppy accounting, ruthless managers, and conflicting egos drive Lou to the brink. He fires Andy Warhol—Lou recalls, "He turned bright red and called me a rat"—and then John Cale, and then himself, claiming, "I plugged into objective reality and got very sick at what I saw." He is twenty-eight years old.

Lou Reed's last performance with the Velvet Underground takes place on August 23, 1970, at the famous Warhol hangout named Max's Kansas City. Playing alongside Lou are Doug Yule, Sterling Morrison, Maureen Tucker, and Billy Yule. Brigid Berlin, the zaftig Warhol superstar, aims her cassette recorder at the stage and hits the record button. Ms. Berlin is fondly remembered by many as the plump, Fifth Avenue–bred Warhol collaborator who lolled around shooting whipped cream into her mouth and amphetamines into her ass, through her jeans, in the 1966 movie *Chelsea Girls.* Brigid's recording of Lou's last performance with the VU is a sacred document. His ragged voice reveals the extent of his mental and physical collapse.

Unbeknownst to the Max's degenerates and drag queens and Brigid, Lou's ma and pa are driving in from Freeport. After the show they pick up their son at the stage door, in front of astonished bandmates, and disappear into the night. Danny Fields recalls surveying the last remnants of the Velvet Underground with theatre critic Donald Lyons, who commented, "Now we will have to call them the Velveteen Underground."

Lou's retreat to his parents' house is a blaring, flashing indicator of the dire state of his psyche. Kids of Lou's generation, and mine, would have done anything rather than hoist the white flag and crawl back home seeking parental succor. His baffled pals speculate that this shocking move might be evidence of a kind of Stockholm syndrome. (This term was not invented until '73 so they would have had to call it something else.) After years of hearing the stories of his electric shock treatments, his pals are horrified to see him walking back into the alleged torture chamber, embracing his tormentors. The reality is that Toby and Sidney love him and believe, yet again, that they are saving his life and his sanity.

According to Bockris's reporting, Lou spends the first forty-eight hours in his boyhood room feeling "sad, moody, amazed at my own dullness." He starts seeing a psychoanalyst. Once Lou begins to function, his dad sets him up in a forty-dollar-a-week typing job in his accounting office. This information, along with other details of Lou's return to Mom and Pop, is exaggerated and proliferated around the world and becomes a poignant thread in the Lou legend. The prevailing narrative is as follows: Lou has had some kind of nervous breakdown. He can no longer live independently. His dad has given him an office gofer job. The myth concludes as follows: Bowie gets wind of this grim situation, scoops up Lou, and drags him into the studio to record the greatest comeback album of all time. The truth, ladies and gents and all those in between, is more nuanced.

When Lou was a kid, he told anyone who would listen that he was going to be a successful rock star. Now, banging away on a sturdy Remington typewriter, he might have lost his confidence, his dignity, his health, his money, his band, and many of his marbles, but he has not lost his rock-star dream.

His girlfriend and future wife Bettye Kronstad, in her memoir titled *Perfect Day*, recalls the situation as follows: "Lou came from a marvelous, supportive family, and going home gave him the safety and security to find himself again." According to Bettye, Lou was compos mentis, as exemplified by the fact that while working for his dad he published several poems in Harvard's illustrious literary magazine *The Harvard Advocate*, in 1971, repackaging himself as follows: "Louis Reed . . . formerly of the Velvet Underground, writes poetry now." Two of the eight poems are VU song lyrics. The most noteworthy submission is titled "The Coach and Glory of Love" and reappears in a re-worked form as the title song of the '75 album *Coney Island Baby*. Why is this interesting? It gives a window into Lou's process of protracted creative noodling, and even at the lowest point of his career, he has retained this poetic mojo.

A word about the young couple.

Bettye first met Lou in 1968, totally by chance, two years prior to the VU split, when she was a student at Columbia. She describes her first glimpse of Lou as follows: "a skinny guy in a blue denim shirt with white mother-of-pearl snaps half un-done, exposing an abundant growth of chest hair. A wide, worn, leather belt was slung low on his narrow hips, holding up his stylishly weathered bellbottoms . . . His hair was in an Afro but a soft curly light brown one, carefully coiffed. He had his thumb hooked over his belt buckle, and the rest of his hand hung down, carefully pointing to his crotch."

In an attempt to express his appreciation for what Bettye describes as her "long-legged fashionably thin Scandinavian blondeness," Lou slaps her on the ass as they enter an elevator. This auspicious encounter takes place on the Columbia cam-pus, where Bettye is studying for a comparative lit degree. Lou is visiting one of his former college roomies, Lincoln Swados, a massive influence on his creative life.

Swados's descent into mental illness previously triggered a subway suicide attempt that left him alive but missing an arm and a leg. At the time of Lou's elevator slap, Swados is studying creative writing and attempting to get his life back after his ghastly ordeal. Swados, who is also pals with Bettye, becomes the improbable matchmaker who connects the slapper and the slappee. The resulting five-year relationship is fraught and doomed but also tinged with sweetness. Lou will write "Perfect Day" to memorialize time they spent together in Central Park.

After Lou quits the Velvets and moves back to Freeport with his folks, Bettye plays a key role in his renaissance. Within a short period of time Lou, often accompanied by Bettye, is making exploratory trips to New York and reconnecting with pals like Danny Fields.

As we contemplate this chapter of Lou's life, it is tempting to ask the following question: Is this the upside of his multiple personality condition? Different Lous can go off in different directions and try different stuff. One of them can lick his wounds in a typing job, while another attempts to construct a happy, conventional life with Bettye, while yet another attempts to jump-start stardom.

Lou befriends music execs Lisa and Richard Robinson. They believe Lou is a genius who is ready for his breakthrough. Richard works for RCA Records. In September 1971 Richard facilitates a meeting with David Bowie, who has just signed with RCA and is getting ready to release *Hunky Dory*. Bowie worships Lou and wants to meet him. Lou is intrigued. Bowie has shoulder-length blond hair, a penchant for wearing frocks, and a wicked pair of mismatched eyeballs. Lou takes Bowie to Max's so Starman can meet another of his idols, Iggy Pop. Danny Fields recalls the spontaneity of this summit as follows: "I brought Iggy to Max's. I woke him up and dragged him out of bed so he could meet Bowie." Everyone is impressed with everyone.

A year and a half after his Velvet Underground exit, Lou—or one or two of his personalities—has a new manager named Dennis Katz and is flying to the UK to make his first solo album, titled *Lou Reed*. In April 1972 this record is released. A collage of Velvet songs played by polished professional musicians from Elton John's band and Yes, this album fails to deliver mega stardom. *Live at Max's Kansas City*, the VU album made by Brigid with a crappy hand-held recording device, gets much better reviews.

Back in New York a deflated Lou is living in a crummy shag-pile-carpeted apartment with Bettye, who is seen with a black eye. One of Lou's nastiest personalities has become a girlfriend abuser. There are contradictions in Lou's nature that are impossible to ignore. He can be sweet and then—cue the shark with the bloody chin—he can make others suffer.

As '72 dawns, glam rock continues to overtake the charts, most especially in the UK. Marc Bolan (whose full majesty will be unfurled in the upcoming glam rock chapter) is already its successful pop princess—T. Rex's *Electric Warrior* was released the previous year—but David Bowie is the more edgy, idiosyncratic rising star on the cusp of a full-on coronation. Many would-be glitter critters are nipping at Bowie's heels. How can he stay on the throne?

According to wife Angie, David feels that Iggy Pop and Lou are his only real competition. He therefore envelops his two idols in his Kansai Yamamoto cape and coopts them into his circle. In short order, he will produce records for both of his idols.

Peter Stanfield agrees with Angie's assessment, adding, "Lou and Iggy had a history that could be appropriated and made use of. The appropriation of the other's charisma . . . this does not diminish Bowie. It takes him up to another level."

In June '72 *The Rise and Fall of Ziggy Stardust and the Spiders from Mars* is released, and there is no longer any doubt who is ruling the planet. Bowie proposes to RCA that he produce Lou's second solo album. They agree because Bowie is now so major that they would happily come to his house and scrub henna stains from the bathroom sink if he asked them to.

After touring to promote the *Lou Reed* solo album, Lou heads to London, where he will spend ten days at Trident Studios recording *Transformer*. I did my time in Soho in the '70s, dressing windows at Aquascutum, purveyors of tweedy clothing to the aristocracy, including the queen, who wore Aquascutum knee-grazing tweed skirts and sweater sets when hiking through the heather with her corgis. (Camp? No question about it.) The flagship store was on Regents Street, but the display studio was located on Brewer Street, just a hop, skip, and a crotchless-panty shop from Trident Studios at 17 Saint Anne's Court, one of the dinky squalid alleyways that crisscross the bohemian chaos of this area.

My main memories of Soho at this time involve the schlepping of window mannequins. We window dressers would regularly cross Brewer Street carrying naked mannequins, our hands gripping the defenseless fiberglass dollies between their legs. Why the crotch grip? If you tried to carry mannequins by their waists, the lower half of the body would inevitably crash to the pavement. Bend down to retrieve the legs, and the arms would fall off, usually breaking the fingers in the process. Before you knew it, the rock-hard wig would be rolling into oncoming traffic. Even in anything-goes Soho this daily mannequin parade brought traffic to a screeching halt and unleashed a cavalcade of bawdy double entendres. "Give her one for me!" "Bet you wish she was a bloke, dontcha?"

Soho was known for sass, sleaze, jazz, Carnaby Street, Italian pastry shops, rent boys, sweatshops, tailor shops, and endless pubs and drinking clubs including Muriel Belcher's famous Colony Room. This establishment was frequented by a Soho-ish mix of bohemian reprobates including Francis Bacon, Lucian Freud, and the Kray brothers. Lesbian Muriel—Christopher Hitchens once described her as "arguably the rudest person in England"—called her clients "Cunty" or "Mary" depending on her mood. I was a habitué of a nearby low-down gay drinking club called the A and B. (None of us knew what it stood for, but there was no shortage of horrid speculations.) An extremely camp Aquascutum colleague who was known as the Duchess was an A and B member and would invite a bunch of Aquascutum gays to join her in a postwork gin and tonic. After an hour's chitchat—I recall spending a lot of time trying to convince the older habitués that I was not "on the game," i.e., a rent boy—I would walk through the smelly back streets of Soho up to Oxford Street to catch my bus, and every night the same exhausted painted lady, on the same corner of Dean Street would ask me, in a thoroughly bored voice, if I would care to enjoy "a night of fun, dearie?" Soho was a wondrous Hogarthian parody of itself.

Today Soho has exactly the same hip-meets-sleaze vibe. Strip clubs like Raymond Revuebar have been replaced by more sex joints, groovy coffee bars, gay pubs, and dildo and leather jockstrap shops. Though Trident subsequently moved to another part of Soho, there is a historic plaque on the wall of the original location that identifies the building as the place where Bowie birthed *Hunky Dory* and *Ziggy*. The plaque is too small to accommodate a mention of *Transformer*. You will be amazed at the low-key facade of this historic building, a modest edifice in a tiny alleyway. It's hard to imagine all that shimmering glamour—to mention nothing of "Hey Jude" and God knows how many other hits—being created in such a dinky-kinky location.

It's fascinating to imagine Lou and his more conventional lady, who many mistook for a stewardess, sailing into the camp and glamour and frivolity of that London circa 1972. Angie Bowie is assigned the task of finding Lou and Bettye somewhere to live. In her memoir Angie claims that Lou was part of a throuple and that two adorable, smiling, angelic bookends accompany them on the house-hunting trips. Who are these mysterious creatures? Specifics are absent from Angie's helter-skelter account. Suffice it to say that anything is possible. This is a very specific moment of gender mayhem. Marc Bolan is acting so nelly that a significant number of people believe he has already gotten the chop. This is a time when you might well name your child Zowie. Dad could wear a twinkle-knit unitard and a feather boa. In 1972 we are all living in a Bowie universe.

Is this a propitious moment for Lou? Possibly. He has looked at the music business from both sides now. He has won and lost and still somehow he's willing to give it another whirl. Why the hell not? After all, what else can he do? Music and poetry are his dual métiers. Armed with a decade of experience and encouraged by the bravado of his new supernova pal Bowie, he is ready to give stardom another shot.

Is Lou shitting his pants? Most likely. He has doubtless come away from his previous experiences with a nice healthy dose of PTSD. He now has a detailed understanding of how precarious and corrosive the music business can be. With experience under his low-slung belt, he now knows enough to be terrified. Re those trousers: Were they the same gray suede ones made for him a few years prior by Betsey Johnson? Quite possibly. After all, he has yet to make the kind of dough that might scream, "*Hey! Let's go shopping at Gucci.*"

David Bowie and Mick Ronson on a public train to Aberdeen, UK, to perform as Ziggy Stardust and the Spiders from Mars.

(Mick Rock, 1973, 2022)

CHAPTER 3

Bowie

When it comes to celebrities, I am not much given to mawkish sentimentality, but David Bowie is my exception. When he died on January 10, 2016, fans took to social media to express their pain. I, along with countless individuals of various stripes, ages, and affinities, shared feelings of connection, sadness, and a profound sense of gratitude. Danny Fields describes the Bowie postmortem as follows: "David is sanctified now. It's wondrous to see."

On that day, I was on a work trip, ensconced in a flashy hotel in Las Vegas. After hearing of Starman's departure, I rummaged through YouTube and seized upon "Lady Grinning Soul." As Bowie crooned his erotic lament, I stared out at the neon orgasms of the Strip, blinging and twinkling in the early morning light, and let my mind wander back through those golden years, gold, whop, whop, whop.

During the '70s Bowie dangled his feather boa from on high, and in dire need of a lifeline, we grabbed on to it. At the very least we caught a rogue feather or two. His flamboyance and creativity and talent lit up the bleak '70s, filling us with a sense of possibility. Bowie, that cultivated intense young dude, became our patron saint. Through our Bowie worship we learned how to accept our super-freaky status and ourselves. He gave us a guide for how to be a defiant, confident misfit, how to take our otherness and use it to our advantage.

Many gays of my generation lived in terror of becoming a sad cliché, a lonely old poofter, knocking back gin and tonics while listening to scratchy recordings of Judy Garland. Bowie opened the door to a world where personal expression was unlimited and all the outsiders and oddballs of the moment—Marc Bolan, Lindsay Kemp, Ava Cherry, Suzi Ronson, Amanda Lear, Cherry Vanilla, Pierre Laroche, Zandra Rhodes, Kansai Yamamoto, William Burroughs, Freddie Burretti, Wayne County, Iggy Pop, Brian Eno—were making noise, making art, and, in many cases, making money. It was more than "Even though you are different, you are okay." It was "You are different, and guess what, that is a colossal advantage, which, if you throw your fascinator into the ring, will enable you to construct a fabulous life."

Yes, he deserved our adulation, but was he really one of us? And was he really gay?

It's January 22, 1972. I'm walking past my local newsagent (magazine stand) in Manchester when I clock Bowie on the cover of *Melody Maker*. There is a fetching photo of my idol—not yet a redhead, but Ziggy is on the rise—which I will add to the growing collection of images I am Scotch-Taping to the wall of the vermin-ridden hovel I share with three girls. We are studying (not very much) psychology. I still can't quite believe I made it this far in the education system.

My academic history was patchy to say the least. At the age of eleven I failed the notorious eleven-plus exam and was sent to the "other" school, the school for kids who are most likely going to become hairdressers, typists, and plumbers. At the age of sixteen we are all booted out into factory jobs and trades. The career advisor lady suggested I become a "tracer," a bloke who spends his days manually copying blueprints. Unable to face this fate, I spent the summer working in a bottle-top factory. No Saint-Tropez for me.

This gave me cash to buy clothes and also proved to be a highly motivating experience. By the end of the summer I had (finally) realized the importance of education and, with the aid of my stellar O-level results, clawed my way into the local grammar school, where I spend the next two years successfully studying for university entrance qualifications, aka A-levels. Sheesh.

In between bouts of academia and the frantic stitching of my own clothes, I explore the Mancunian gay scene. I am attempting to paint myself into the picture. There's one problem. The picture is not quite as glam and upbeat as I might have desired. The university has a Gay Lib society, but the queens who attend the meetings are—bless them!—somewhat ethereal. They worship Erik Satie,* and they play the dulcimer. They sit on each other's knees, knitting incredibly long scarves or reading Tolkien. They are—no, really, bless them!—a warm-up for the Radical Faeries, who would emerge later in the decade. (Bless them too!!) Being a regular hippie was, back then, already quite gay enough. Being a gay hippie was a great way to meet an untimely end, most likely at the hands of the Manchester skinheads, of which there was an abundance.

So I check out the city's gay bars, and find them cheery and welcoming but filled with tart-tongued pill-popping young queens,

* Yes, the author of the marathon piano piece played by Cale and Cage. Satie was a Montmartre eccentric circa 1900 whose fabulously tight-assed music enjoyed a revival during the hippie era. He wore velvet suits and drank himself to death. I knew some gay hippies who would dance on his grave every year on the anniversary of his death.

many of whom seem to be taking more than just a walk on the wild side. Their "boyfriends" are older queens who secretly drink Dr. J. Collis Browne's tonic out of tiny bottles.* The youngsters are known as daughters and the old queens are mothers. When you walk into one of the bars down by the Manchester canals, all you can hear are shrieks of "Mother! Buy us a gin and tonic!" or "Buy it yourself, daughter!"

Between the winsome university fairies and the scrappy working-class mothers and daughters, I struggle to find an entry point into the dolce vita of Manchester gay life. The answer is lurking in my hot little hands, in that *Melody Maker*, in an explosive interview with my idol.

"David's present image is to come on like a swishy queen, a gorgeously effeminate boy. He's as camp as a row of tents, with his limp hand and trolling vocabulary. 'I'm gay,' he says, 'and always have been, even when I was David Jones.' But there's a sly jollity about how he says it, a secret smile at the corners of his mouth. He knows that in these times it's permissible to act like a male tart, and that to shock and outrage, which pop has always striven to do throughout its history, is a ball-breaking process. And if he's not an outrage, he is, at the least, an amusement. 'Why aren't you wearing your girl's dress today?' I said to him (he has no monopoly on tongue-in-cheek humour). 'Oh dear,' he replied. 'You must understand that it's not a woman's. It's a man's dress.'" Interviewer Michael Watts is referring to the "dresses for men"

---

* Dr. J. Collis Browne's compound was an addictive opium-laced "tonic" that came in small sinister brown-glass bottles and was abused by degenerate oldsters looking for an unregulated high.

designed by Michael Fish.* Bowie wore a fetching example on the back cover of *Hunky Dory*, and Mick Jagger sported a short white version two years prior at a concert in Hyde Park, which paid tribute to Stones founder Brian Jones after he drowned in his swimming pool at the age of twenty-seven.

Having someone like Bowie admit to being gay and act in such a recklessly, hilariously camp manner is revolutionary. Bowie is a bloke, like me, from a crap town, who is broadcasting his queerness. And he is not cringing in a corner. He is powerful, creative, and wildly original, and he gets to make music, and wear dresses designed by Michael Fish. And he's not angry or self-loathing. He is amusing himself by toying with the interviewer. In short: he's fucking fabulous.

Bowie is, and always has been, very amusing. He likes to banter. Yes, he is book smart and self-cultivated, but he remains very much the South London lad, enjoying taking the piss, always charming and self-deprecating in that British way. And he loves to give the press the old windup. In July 1972, at the Dorchester press conference for the kickoff of his Ziggy tour—Iggy and Lou are in attendance—Bowie declares the following:

"People like Lou and I are probably predicting the end of

------

* Michael Fish was an English dandy who worked, as did I, for mega-posh shirtmaker Turnbull & Asser on Jermyn Street, where Michael famously invented the new wider "kipper tie." Back in the mid-'70s I was the head, and only, window dresser. After leaving T & A, Michael opened his own store, purveying the most flamboyant menswear in history, including the aforementioned "dresses for men." #legend

an era, and I mean that catastrophically. Any society that allows people like Lou and me to be rampant is pretty well lost. We're both very mixed-up paranoid people—absolute walking messes. I don't really know what we're doing. If we're the spearhead of anything, we're not necessarily the spearhead of anything good." I can only imagine how literally and seriously this was taken by US journalists. *Oh my gaaaahhhhd! These boys are total nihilists!!!*

I later would have the good fortune to banter with Bowie on several occasions.

Sidebar: I moved from London to Los Angeles in 1977 and lived *la vie bohème* and never saw hide nor hair of Bowie—he loathed LA—until 1983, when he played the Forum during his Serious Moonlight Tour, promoting the album *Let's Dance*. This is the beginning of a commercial period Bowie would subsequently refer to as "my Phil Collins period."

I remember two things about this concert. First, there is Bowie's new incarnation as snake-hipped, suited, blond matinee idol, swiveling around the stage like a cobra in a Saville Row suit.

The second thing I remember is infinitely more horrible. I attend the concert with two best friends, Mundo and Jef. Two days prior I had accompanied Mundo to the doctor, where he was diagnosed with AIDS, the "gay cancer," as it is still called. The lump on his neck is Kaposi's sarcoma. When I asked the doctor for a referral he replied, "There are no referrals. There is no cure. Are you boys religious?" There was no talk of getting AIDS tested. And since there are no treatments on offer, what would be the point? Better to go for a swim with rocks in your pockets, or overdose on heroin.

I am sick with worry about Mundo but also paralyzed with

anxiety about myself. Since the doctor visit I have barely slept. Mundo and I were in a relationship before he moved on to Jef, so clearly I am next for the chopping block. Gripped by a ghastly sense of foreboding, I stare at my hands, waiting for lesions to appear. While Bowie slithers around the stage, I play out a grim future in my head in which we all die horrible deaths. Mundo and Jef, meanwhile, are joking and laughing and sharing a doobie and rocking out to Bowie with commendable abandon. I am mute. All I can think about is the death and suffering to come.

All my forebodings came true. An entire swath of our gorgeous gay pals were wiped out, dying horrible, painful deaths. Whenever I hear "Let's Dance," I think, *Yes, dance if you dare, the dance of death.*

Mundo Meza died in 1985, aged thirty. His paintings have recently become much sought after. Jef Huereque is—thank the Lord!—very much alive, making art and living in Los Angeles.

In 1985, not long after Mundo died, I move to New York City, which is, by then, Bowie's hometown. Working at Barneys, I establish a reputation for my outré window displays. It is a fabulous, all-consuming gig, one that affords me a few hours of daily therapeutic escape from the death that is ravaging my peers, until the grim reaper comes for me.

I join Act Up and spend many weekends spray-mounting "Silence = Death" posters onto foamcore. My job consumes me. I collaborate with various artists on my window displays, including Warhol, Basquiat, Haring, and Rauschenberg. Window displays are a cultural thing in the '80s, the Instagram of the era. AIDS testing becomes a thing. I trudge to a public clinic in the Chelsea projects, near Barneys. Three weeks later I schlepp my way back, on my lunch hour, to get the results.

It's well over a year before I can wrap my head around my negative result. There is no good reason why I have dodged the grim reaper. I have not been a tramp, but I have not been Rebecca of Sunnybrook Farm either.

Back to Bowie.

I first meet Bowie at a Barneys–*Vanity Fair* window-unveiling party in 1990. I tell him I am a huge fan and that I attended the '72 Finsbury Park Rainbow Theatre concert. He replies, "Oh, I am a huge fan of yours. I especially enjoyed your Tammy Faye Bakker window." *Bloody hell!!! You're a fan of mine?* For Barneys holiday windows I had, in one particular tableau, chosen to memorialize Tammy Faye, the lachrymose TV evangelist, creating a satirical vignette loaded with inside jokes and quips. Bowie was very entertained.

Subsequently Bowie loans me stuff for my window displays, including the extraordinary half-incinerated Union Jack flared coat that Alexander McQueen created for him for his tour with Nine Inch Nails. Barneys, my employer, throws a party at Indochine for Bowie and Alexander. It is a small but memorable soirée. Bowie, who lives down the street, arrives, all glammed up and hennaed, twirling the panels of the McQueen coat. He is a delight and expends his energies making sure Alexander, a shy bloke, is put at ease and that everyone has a smashing time.

One night I run into Bowie and his wife, Iman, and their daughter, who is in a stroller, promenading on University Place. In *David Bowie: The Oral History*, author Dylan Jones describes Iman as follows: "Iman Mohamed Abdulmajid married David Bowie on April 24, 1992. Incontestably, she was the love of his life, bringing him calm, stability, and newfound passion for life." We are pals. She is every bit as magnificent as she appears. Iman is blessed with a wicked sense of humor and can banter with the best.

On this occasion, David is buying ciggies at the local deli. I fail to clock the Bowie family at first because they are wearing schlumpy clothes—a cunning street disguise—and are passing unnoticed. My bloke Jonathan and I introduce the group to our new dog, explaining that his name is Liberace. David makes a valiant and hilarious attempt to explain to his daughter who Liberace was, and why this is a noteworthy name choice for a tough, butch little terrier.

I always felt an additional bond with Bowie because we both grew up with more than our fair share of, what were referred to back then as, lunatics. Bowie had a schizophrenic side to his family tree and no shortage of suicides. My family had a similar story. After my grandfather shot himself, my gran began to lose her marbles. She was institutionalized, diagnosed as schizo, given a lobotomy, and then sent to live with us. My uncle Ken, her son, was also schizophrenic. He also resided chez nous. Like Lou, he suffered through electric shock treatment and came home in a daze. As with Bowie, the proximity to all this madness left me with a lifelong fear of losing my mind. Since homosexuality was defined as a mental illness, I already felt I was halfway there.

Bowie's drive came from a desire to outrun this schizo destiny. In that oral history by Dylan Jones, Bowie says the following: "Because of the tragedy inflicted, especially on my mother's side of the family, there were too many suicides for my liking—that was something I was terribly fearful of." He describes how he attempted to avoid madness by putting all his "psychological excesses" into his music. My drive, though clearly less impressive than Bowie's, had similar origins. Lou's demons, on the other hand? They seemed to percolate from within. No batty relatives to blame. His demons were already part of him. Outrunning them was most likely not an option.

August 1972. Bowie's coronation year. The two lads, along with Mick Ronson, descend on Trident Studios in Soho. Will they end up killing each other? Will Bowie's good humor withstand Lou's mood swings? Is this the right move for the greatest songwriter of his age? Will anyone be able to understand Mick Ronson, who has one of the thickest UK regional accents since Eric Burden of the Animals? There are several reasons for optimism.

Propelled by an enthusiasm for the emerging London sound, Lou is jonesing to cross the Atlantic. Lou and Bowie have stuff in common. They both are poetic dudes who read books. They both have been knocking themselves out for a decade to become rock stars. And, most important, they both are huge fans of . . . Lou Reed. Lou has a big ego, and Bowie is smart enough to give it some leash. Bowie's lightness—he sees things through the lens of camp, humor, satire, theatricality—will hopefully be a good foil for Lou's grim self-seriousness. Fingers crossed.

Those still clinging to the old saw that Bowie saved Lou from the dystopian hell of his dad's dreary office need to let go of that theory. Like I said. It's more straightforward. *Transformer* is a work of symbiosis. Everyone needs everyone. Everyone benefits. Despite his explosive success, Bowie needs the edgy vibe and the whiff of the avant-garde—the DNA of the Velvet Underground that Lou brings. As Lou reportedly later recalls, "David learned how to be hip. Associating with me brought his name out to a lot more people." Glam rock is spreading like wildfire, and Bowie needs to build a firewall between himself and the more quotidian pop glam glitter critters who are scampering up the charts. God forbid they should catch up with him.

Lou wants to be a rock star. He wants hits and money and the whole shebang. And he could also use a good laugh. The failure of his first solo album lingers. There is a lightness to Bowie's London that is not part of the New York scene. London is (cheap) champagne and New York is smack. All the morose, moody introspection of the Velvet Underground . . . where did it get him? Why not try switching gears? Pass the mascara.

Bettye Kronstad, the soon-to-be Mrs. Reed, recalls the *Transformer* interlude as "one of the most enjoyable periods of our relationship." Though her main role is making sure Lou's addictive impulses are monitored so that he can fulfill his commitments, they manage to cram in some glamorous diversions. Days are spent shopping on Portobello Road, followed by evenings at the theatre, followed by socializing with other happening pop personalities, including Dusty Springfield, Petula Clark, and Lulu. The trip cements their relationship. As per Bettye's account, upon returning to NYC Lou drags her off to buy an engagement ring. Which brings us back to an important question: Since Bowie has a wife and a kid (Angie and Zowie), and Bettye and Lou are picking out engagement rings, exactly *how gay are these boys?*

Bowie's marriage plays a significant role in buffering him against negativity. In Sasha Geffen's smashing book *Glitter Up the Dark: How Pop Music Broke the Gender Binary*, she notes that Bowie's "flamboyant performance was ultimately grounded in the reassuring symbol of the heterosexual nuclear family." She also notes, "His cis masculinity gave many listeners—and record executives—a sense of plausible deniability." So, are Bowie and Lou for real? Or is it just a marketing tactic? Are they really gay?

I keep putting off answering this question, but now my back is against the wall. I am at the end of the chapter. Here's the way I see it: Bowie and Lou both toyed with effeminacy, bisexuality, and homosexuality, reaping advantages and disadvantages along the way. They successfully used these radioactive modes—they sucked each other's faces in front of journalists—to propel and shape their fame and image. They were not, in my opinion, indulging in cynical exploitation.

The early '70s was a period when sexual liberation collided with unisex style and androgyny. Amanda Lear, model, enigma, chanteuse, and Bowie collaborator and paramour, epitomized the fluid nature of sexuality during this era. Though it is generally assumed she is a trans woman, Amanda has deftly never clarified the situation. I vividly remember dancing next to her—she was wearing a black rubber catsuit—at El Sombrero. That's Amanda, shot by Karl Stoecker, prowling with a panther, on the cover of the Roxy Music *For Your Pleasure*. Her disco hit "Follow Me" would later become a gay anthem.

Amanda describes her affair with Bowie in her memoir *My Life with Dalí*. Their trysts, chez Amanda, were frequently interrupted by a complicit Angie calling to ask, "Good morning, darling. Could I speak to my husband? Thank you." Angie would take Amanda lingerie shopping, buying her items that David might enjoy. According to Amanda, Bowie also kept a boyfriend—most likely his costume maker Freddie Burretti, aka Rudi Valentino—in their basement pied-à-terre.

For moi, the soundtrack of this era was "Love the One You're With," the Stephen Stills song recorded by so many, including the Isley Brothers and Aretha Franklin. Lou and Bowie flung contradictions in every direction and loved the ones they were with.

A month after the release of *Transformer* the *New York Times* published an article by Henry Edwards titled "Freak Rock Takes Over." Though Edwards gives *Transformer* a lacerating review, he does underscore the benefits of all this sexual fluidity and ambiguity: "The refusal to declare whether one is a man or woman or the insistence that one can be both is certainly a powerful swipe at middle-class convention. That swipe becomes even more powerful as rock audiences begin to accept declared homosexuals and bisexuals and performing transvestites as their stars. Add to this those staged episodes of violence and mayhem and the result, titillating and repellent at the same time, becomes a neatly packaged message of defiance the rock audience can send home, using the sensation-seeking media as its very own carrier pigeon."

With their freewheeling fluidity and flexibility Bowie and Lou were sending messages home and changing the culture. They were very much a harbinger of today's young gender warriors who describe themselves as pansexual, fluid, nonbinary, or queer identified. Bowie and Lou were, in other words, simply ahead of their time.

All the glitter of Marc Bolan of T-Rex at the Sundown in Edmonton, London, in December 1972.

(Michael Putland/Getty Images)

CHAPTER 4

Glam Rock

With their face sucking and their provocative statements, Bowie and Lou are making my aunt Maud very nervous. I don't actually have an aunt Maud, but if I did she would be quaking in her knee-highs, and not just about the sex stuff. It's the appearance, the decadent costumery of these lads, that are freaking her the fuck out.

Clothing is nonverbal communication. Your choice of blouse tells people like aunt Maud, and others, a great deal about who you are, way before you have even opened your trap. When people see me coming down the street in my flowery mod shirt and velvet jacket, they know immediately that they are gawking at a dedicated follower of fashion, a gay, an aesthete, somebody who is still clinging desperately to the ideals of the Swinging Sixties. So, if clothing is nonverbal communication, what the hell does early '70s glam rock say about the wearer?

First maybe a little definition or two is in order. What makes glam rock, glam rock? Andy Warhol once described himself in an interview with the *East Village Other* as "deeply superficial." The same might be said of glam rock.

Glam rock music, developed mostly in the UK in the early '70s, was a rejection of the earnestness in progressive rock, replacing it with decadence, and infantile FUN. Glam rock was nostalgic, a glorious mash-up of '50s rock and roll, bubblegum pop, and anything else that was handy, including science fiction and cabaret. If this sounds confusing, I am not surprised. It was a confusing era. As cultural commentator Paul Gorman describes it, "The '60s were linear. The maxi followed the mini. Narrow ties and pants were followed by kipper ties and flares. Mod made way for hippie. This was fast-moving but nonetheless it was also a recognizable action/ reaction fashion cycle. The '70s remain more difficult to unpick because everything happened at once: Downtown glam and the testing of gender identity boundaries coincided with uptown haute couture, punk clashed with disco. It was chaos, beautiful chaos."

Tim Blanks, glam-rocking in the Antipodes, recalls to me the empowering nature of glam rock: "Glam rock was an incredible amount of fun. It felt like something that belonged to us. There were probably six of us in Auckland. We could be complete freaks, nightmarishly confident teenagers causing havoc. Glam rock was an incredible license to be you and foolish and fabulous, to be the devoted fan rather than the detached onlooker. There were all those hippies and then there was us."

As with glam rock music, glam rock sartorial style is a reaction to the self-seriousness of hippie culture. Glam rock hauls you out of your geodesic dome home in Topanga Canyon, tears off your dashiki and patched denims, kidnaps you, and drives you to Las Vegas for a showbiz makeover. The sincerity of Woodstock style is superseded by high-voltage theatrical costumery. Hollywood Busby Berkeley glamour collides with showmanship, Disney, gender ambiguity, kitsch, sci-fi, and general exhibitionism. Glam rock = deeply superficial.

And what, then, does glam rock style say about the wearer?

Glam rock is a high-pitched warning screech. Glam rock says, "Caution: The person in front of you is either a rock star or an attention-seeking, self-dramatizing maniac, or both." Noted culture scribe Nik Cohn, writing in *Harpers & Queen* in 1973 in a piece titled "Glamour Is a Dream Machine," describes glamour as follows: "A triumphant return to freakishness, decadence, insanity; lots of violence, swilled down with a dash of perversity; early and melodramatic death where possible, or at least a glut of suffering." Cue the sequins.

Lou Reed's interpretation of glam rock style is less audacious than Bowie's but nonetheless arresting. It's a tarted-up version of his street-punk, black shades, black T-shirt look, but with painted nails and gobs of makeup. "When I saw Lou Reed perform in London in the summer of 1972, the influence of Bowie's theatrical, sexually ambiguous aesthetic was apparent; Lou wore black eye makeup, black lipstick, and a black velvet suit with rhinestone trimmings," remembers Ellen Willis of *The New Yorker*. As per Ms. Willis, a seasoned Lou watcher, "The album *Transformer* referred directly and explicitly to gay life and transvestism. The subject matter was not new, but Lou's attitude toward it was—he was now openly identifying with a subculture he had always viewed obliquely, from a protective, ironic distance." He is no longer waving from the shore. He's thrashing about, caught in a riptide.

When *Transformer* is released in November '72, adorned with the high-contrast Mick Rock portrait, Lou becomes known as the Phantom of Rock. This new look is seen as a provocation. People get their glam panties in a knot over his style switch.

Does Lou have any options? What else could he wear? The truth is that glam rock is, during that heady time in the early 1970s, peak pandemic. Were Lou to have sidestepped the trend and continued sporting his usual street-punk look, he would have been virtually invisible onstage, or more likely mistaken for a roadie.

Prior to Bowie and Lou, glam rock was a Bolan thing. In 1968 Marc Bolan and Mickey Finn formed a band called Tyrannosaurus Rex. Bring on the goblins and pixies. Their particular genre was a mash-up of fairy stories and psychedelia, as exemplified by the title—surely the fay-est and longest in history—of their debut album: *My People Were Fair and Had Sky in Their Hair . . . But Now They're Content to Wear Stars on Their Brows.* In 1970 Mickey and Marc ditched the wizards and fairies, donned glitter-encrusted platform boots, and began pumping out glam hit after catchy hit: "Ride a White Swan," "Hot Love," "Get It On (Bang a Gong)," "Jeepster," "Telegram Sam," "Metal Guru," and more. Bolan's '50s-influenced rock—slicing and chopping guitars, hand clapping, and surfer bongos—epitomized glam rock pop. In his sequins, boas, and fluffy sweaters, Bolan vamped and pouted his way into megastardom. The album *Electric Warrior*, which preceded *The Rise and Fall of Ziggy Stardust* by nine months, remains a personal favorite.

Bowie and Bolan had been friends since their early mod days. The first-wave London mods were sexually ambiguous working-class dandies and often wore makeup. As George Melly notes in his nifty book *Revolt into Style*, "There was admittedly a strong homosexual element involved—but it was not so much overt homosexuality as narcissistic. Girls were irrelevant. The little Mods used each other as looking glasses. They were as cool as ice-cubes." Enter Bolan and Bowie.

According to Bowie—I got this directly from the horse's mouth—he and Bolan developed their fashion sense while rummaging together through the discards dumped nightly in the garmento trash cans around Soho and Carnaby Street, the mod epicenter of London. According to UK glam rock lore, a stylish genius named Chelita Secunda, wife of Bolan manager Tony Secunda, clocking Bolan's dinky physique and general prettiness, propelled the former mod into High Street girls' shops where she festooned him in boas, satin, and girly accessories, thereby "inventing glam rock" and transforming Bolan into an avatar of the coming glitter revolution. Bolan's subsequent runaway success preceded Bowie's and must have been quite motivating/alarming to Bowie. As Bolan's manager Simon Napier-Bell recalls in Dylan Jones's *David Bowie: The Oral History*, "All artists are deadly rivals even when they are presenting not to be. Bowie and Bolan were no different."

However, Bolan's fizzy pop-princess genre allowed plenty of space for Roxy Music and Bowie and Lou and Iggy to provide a thinking man's version of glam rock, more Velvet Underground inspired. Since Bolan played guitar on Bowie's 1970 single "The Prettiest Star" and supplied backup on "Heroes," recorded in 1977, it seems fair to assume that they remained friends. Future rivalries were eliminated when, a week after the release of the *Heroes* album, Bolan died in a car smashup. Flowers and fans memorialize the crash site to this day.

So Bolan occupied center stage in the first thrust of mainstream glam rock—the pop bubblegum, '50s rock and roll version—inspiring a stampede of pop glitter critters, including Gary Glitter, Alvin Stardust, Sweet, Mud, Slade, and, another Bowie protégé band, Mott the Hoople.

Glam rock even influenced the clothing of non–glam rock artists like Elton John and Rod Stewart, who around this time started calling each other Sharon and Phyllis, respectively. (God bless the Brits for their willingness to be silly.) Glam rock did not quite get the traction in the US, Lou and Alice Cooper being the only major artists to enjoy glam hits. Others who toyed with the genre, whilst remaining doggedly true to rock and roll, include the New York Dolls, Suzi Quatro, Sparks, and Iggy Pop.

History will always elevate Bolan, Bowie, Lou, and Iggy over the other glamdrogynists. As author Peter Stanfield eloquently puts it in his book *Pin Ups 1972*, these four were "performers who worked on and then blurred the line between pop and art, artifice and authenticity, surface and depth, fantasy and reality, the plebeian and the noble."

My own plebeian glam rock journey was exclusively sartorial—I was a happy consumer of the music and never had the impulse to produce it—and began at a boutique named Mr Freedom, the brainchild of a portly legend named Tommy Roberts. In his two stores, one located on Kensington High Street and the other King's Road, Tommy created a world of satin and stars and cartoony madness. Mr Freedom clothing was knowing, ironic, and—this is going to sound insane—very thoughtful and sophisticated. It was pop art rather than glitter trash, so the emphasis was on satin and velvet, rather than tacky showbiz fabrics like lamé and brocade. My friend Pam was one of the in-house designers at Mr Freedom. While working there she officially changed her name to Pamla Motown. Everything at Mr Freedom was similarly playful and camp. We're talking rainbow knits and leggings; velvet jackets in yellow and blue, top-stitched in red; polka-dot printed satin jackets and rompers; and long-sleeve T-shirts embellished with satin appliqués of stars, rainbows, and Goofy and Mickey. Tommy was the first person on Earth to license Disney imagery and place it in a fashion context. Whenever a '60s rocker auctions his old stuff—I am thinking of the recent Bill Wyman auction—there is always a cluster of gems from Mr Freedom.

Who shopped at Mr Freedom? A huge range of people, including Mick Jagger, Jean Shrimpton, Twiggy, and Yves Saint Laurent, plus anyone with a sense of humor and the impulse to be seen. The prices, unlike those of today's demented designer offerings, were non-exclusionary. Working-class kids spending their factory earnings rubbed shoulders with pop stars, art students blowing their grant money, hairdressers, and flashy shop assistants from other stores. Tweedy aristocrats stayed away in droves. The gays? We'll get to them in a moment.

I had neither the money nor the balls to go full bore at Mr Freedom, but I dabbled with sweaters and baggy high-waisted pants. What I could not afford I whipped together myself. The most iconic Mr Freedom item was the satin souvenir jacket, a zippered blouson that resembled a varsity or jockey jacket, in contrasting colors. I found a dressmaker pattern for this style of jacket, bought a yard of electric-blue satin and a yard of white, some elastic, and I sewed it myself on an Edwardian Singer sewing machine that I had taken with me to college. If you turned my jacket inside out, it was a home-sewn disaster of pinked seams and dangling threads, but the exterior was ferocious, which was all that mattered. Glam rock style was about appearances. As the Brits say, "It was all fur coat and no knickers."

Lacking the requisite cobbler skills, I was unable to fabricate my own shoes or space boots—I would drool over the Terry de Havilland platforms, with their stars and sunbursts, in Kensington Market—so I was forced to look elsewhere. But fate had smiled on me. Thanks to the malnutrition of the postwar era, I was, like a lot of those dinky mods, born undersized, including my feet. Like petite Marc Bolan, I could wear women's shoes and boots, which were inexpensive and came in more adventurous styles than high-street men's shoes.

I recall a blue metallic pair of scaled up children's sandals with two-and-half-inch-thick soles. The pièce de résistance of my collection was a pair of navy-blue lace-up Bata women's shoes—the ones I wore to the Finsbury Park Rainbow—with a two-inch platform and a five-inch heel. The upside? I was now five feet nine inches tall. The downside: I nearly broke my neck falling downstairs on two separate occasions. Fortunately I was plastered both times so I was relaxed and broke no bones. Now designers like Rick Owens offer platform shoes for men. I am not tempted. Being average height one more time before I die would be exhilarating, but I might feel a bit tragic. I can imagine the thought bubbles on the street: *Ah! Look at the little fella trying to be tall.* Whereas, back in the day, the platform trend was so de rigueur that the thought bubbles were more generous: *Oh, look at the fashionable little fella! Now he's normal height thanks to this new trend.*

Glam rock was, in addition to being a music thing, very much a style thing, a store-hopping fashion-exhibitionist thing, especially in the UK. When the brilliant Nick Kent later disdainfully described *Transformer* as "exquisite muzak for King's Road boutiques," he was, from my vantage point, paying a massive compliment.

While I was cobbling together my look in Manchester, Tim Blanks was similarly occupied down under: "Glam rock was about the deliciousness of getting tarted up. I had a self-styled Ziggy look, in a leopard Lurex bolero, pedal pushers, lipstick, and rouge. I dyed my hair red and razor-cut the sides. I had a T-shirt made of the *Transformer* cover, and once when I was wearing it, somebody said, 'Is that you?' I was walking on air!"

Glam rock was not a club thing. This was all happening pre–disco explosion so there was a dearth of nocturnal gathering spots. It was about strutting down the boulevard and then popping into a live music venue. You wore your groovy glam rags to see Bolan or Bowie or Roxy Music. There were a few trendy gay clubs in London, like El Sombrero, where you might find one or two like-minded souls. At the height of the glam rock trend, one simply staggered to the local pub and gave all the old pensioners a big laugh.

I have a vivid memory of glam-rocking at the local gay pub in my hometown. My best pal James Biddlecombe and I, total Bowie-aholics, were working at the local department store, him permanently, me during my college summer break.* I flicked a feather duster in "clocks and watches" and Biddie was the queen of "soft furnishings." With his hennaed toilet-brush coiffure and long neck he was a dead ringer for Ziggy. Customers would ask, "Are you David Bowie?" as if the emperor of glam rock might have nothing better to do on a Saturday afternoon than measure yards of damask and chintz for old ladies in a department store, which, by the way, was a dead ringer for the dusty emporium depicted in the legendary comedy series *Are You Being Served?* Gay kids of my generation definitely needed a bestie. We were each other's. At the time of writing, Biddie and I are both still alive. Miraculous.

We were feral and rowdy. In order to keep boredom at bay we

---

* James "Biddie" Biddlecombe went on to become a noteworthy performer on the London club scene. His drag act, which he performed at trans legend April Ashley's club in London and at many other venues, involved switching out a series of elaborate hats. Later, he and his singing partner, Eve Ferret, who had a featured role in the movie *Absolute Beginners*, alongside Bowie, lit up the stage of the legendary Blitz Club, where Biddie ditched the drag in favor of gold lamé suits. In later years he became a beloved pantomime dame. Pantomime: a traditional holiday staged entertainment—bawdy and idiotic, often collaging Gilbert and Sullivan characters into the mix—that is enjoyed by the British public during the festive season. Cross-dressing has been a big part of panto for centuries. Biddie's Widow Twankey was the stuff of legend.

elected to introduce the local gay bar to a little satin 'n' tat. The Railway Tavern, located between the train station and the abattoir, had a "functions room." Every other Friday night was—*pssst!*—gay night. Entering this establishment was nerve-racking and usually entailed walking round the block several times. If you saw somebody you knew, you just kept walking. God forbid an acquaintance might observe you entering the Railway Tavern, put two and two together, and then tell Cyril and Doreen or Betty and Terry, our long-suffering parents, what we were up to.

Biddie and I were well aware that this joint was extremely naff, but that was the whole point. We would grace the Railway Tavern functions room with our presence safe in the knowledge that it would afford us the opportunity to assert our stylish superiority. #slumming. We might've been working-class misfits, but we were confident working-class misfits. And we knew naff when we saw it.

"Naff" was the most important word in the gay vocabulary back then. It was used to describe anything that was, shall we say, less than fabulous. The derivation is fascinating. Apparently it started as an acronym that was used by gay men to describe attractive-but-unavailable heterosexual men: Not Available For Fucking; i.e., straight. When homosexuality was verboten, the word "naff" provided a useful shorthand. Time marched on, and by the time I came of age, homosexuality was newly legal, and the word "naff" was being applied to anything and everything ("Those curtains are sooo naff!") that one might deem unstylish, conventional, and therefore unacceptable. "Naff" became an established part of the famous gay Polari lexicon.

This might be an appropriate moment to digress and point out that half a century ago we gays still had our own secret language: Polari. What Yiddish was to the Jews, Polari was to the gays, albeit on a much smaller scale. We could communicate with each other covertly. Todd Haynes authenticated his glam rock movie *Velvet Goldmine* by introducing Polari speakers and thoughtfully providing subtitles. Biddie and I learned Polari from the older queens at the department store and from listening to a Sunday BBC radio show where, shockingly, two screaming queens called Julian and Sandy would Polari their brains out sans any explanation. Heaven knows what regular listeners made of it all.

Here's an example of a typical Polari sentence: "Vada the bona homie with the naff T-shirt. Bona eek, nante riah, but exquisite lallies, and vada the silky ogle-riahs!" Translation: "Check out the gorgeous guy in the gnarly T-shirt. Handsome face, terrible hair, but gorgeous legs, and check out the silky eyelashes." It's vaguely reminiscent of the lingo spoken by the psychopathic youth in Kubrick's movie *A Clockwork Orange*. See also the original book by Anthony Burgess.

Polari's origins can be traced to the circus and thence to the theatre, where Romany and Italian phrases were absorbed and mangled into a lexicon that was adopted and modified by the gays of yore who were in dire need of a secret language. I am happy to report that I have old pals with whom I still Polari. It's nice to keep the old traditions alive.

So Biddie and I are holding our noses as we prepare to enter this naff establishment. I cannot remember exactly what we were wearing, but I know that wide-legged Oxford bag trousers and platform shoes are involved. I am definitely sporting the homemade satin jockey jacket. Once the coast is clear, we dive in through the side door and disappear into the hell of the functions room, where the smell of smoke and Aramis hits us like a breaking wave. Biddie and I bypass the bar—we already drank a fifth of gin in an alleyway—and immediately descend on the DJ and demand that he play "Suffragette City." He doesn't have it—God, this homie is naff!—so we content ourselves with whatever is on the turntable, which was probably an old-school showbiz gem. Rolling our eyeballs at the naffness of the ambience, we fling ourselves onto the dance floor and do our classic Bowie moves— Biddie can do that thing where he makes spectacles out of his upside-down fingers—whilst wielding our cigarette holders. Yes, you read correctly. We had just seen pics of Bowie rocking a cigarette holder and had added this accessory to our repertoire. Biddie swings his ciggie in a huge arc and—*quel horreur*—burns a long hole in the stretch lacey nylon shirt of one of the older habitués. After the audible screech of pain, all hell breaks loose. Commenting on the naffness of the damaged garment only pours fuel on the fire, and we are asked to leave and told not to come back. What's my point? Brace yourselves. It's a profound one riddled with paradox: the gays were not especially into glam rock.

The most astonishing thing about glam rock—the style and the music—was its aggressive heterosexuality. The key figures were blokey and horny and enjoyed a smoldering female fan base. What could be straighter than Slade, who were, formerly, a bunch of bovver-boot-wearing skinheads? There was ambiguity with Lou and Bowie, but UK pop superstar Alvin Stardust, with his three wives and four kids? Danny Fields recalls the New York Dolls— the most shockingly dragtastic band of all time—as "five of the straightest people I ever knew."

It's hard to think of a prominent gay bloke embracing glam rock style, other than Elton, who was not even out of the closet at the time. Glam rock was too gay for the gays. Freddie Mercury— the only real gay for miles—dabbled, but in a butch biker way. The prominent blokes who careened into glam drag were disappointingly straight. Or as we would have said back then, "She's Arthur, not Martha."

And what about regular people? Non-musicians? Civilians? Again it was the straights who led the charge. Glam rock came too soon for the grown-up gays, who had only recently been "legalized." Only idiotic young fashion exhibitionists like me and Biddie were reckless enough to take it on. Otherwise it was the straight lads. In my interview with Paul Gorman, he explains the straight-glam axis as follows: "It gave straight boys an opportunity to dress out. School kids would be kicking a ball wearing platform shoes. It was an opportunity to piss off the parents and challenge the beer boys."

Glam rock was highly influential and can be seen in subsequent style and music trends. During the New Romantic era—Adam Ant, Pete Burns, Marilyn, Boy George, Spandau Ballet, Steve Strange, and Visage—a new style proliferated, which took glam rock into a costumey world of aristocrats and pirates, all jabots and chopines. Louis Quatorze meets Jack Sparrow.

New Romantic was succeeded by the straightest and yet most flamboyant genre of all time. Paging Twisted Sister! The Hair Metal revolution of the '80s, another direct descendent of glam rock, featured testosterone-riddled straight guys—Mötley Crüe, Def Leppard, Guns N' Roses, Bon Jovi, Poison, et al.—wearing flowing silk scarves, lurid-colored spandex, turquoise leather scrunch boots, and torrents of moussed curls and gobs of mascara. Think Joan Cusack in *Working Girl*. Though clearly in touch with their feminine sides in some way or other, these boys were horny and hairy-chested and hetero. Not a poof amongst them.

The one out-and-proud exception to the hetero-glam monopoly of American music was an American gay whose stage name was Jobriath. The sexual ambiguity promoted by Bowie and Lou—Arthur or Martha? Boris or Doris?—left a void into which came skipping this mysterious creature. "I'm rock's truest fairy. Asking me if I'm homosexual is like asking James Brown if he's black," declared Bruce Wayne Campbell, aka Jobriath, who was destined to become the Fyre Festival of glam rock artists. He was the first openly gay performer to be signed to a record label, soon becoming glam rock's gay cautionary tale. The run-up to his colossally overhyped launch—post-*Transformer*, early '70s—included global advertising and a massive billboard in Times Square. I remember seeing the ads for Jobriath—lipsticked, naked, and reclining—in all the music papers and Andy Warhol's *Interview* magazine.

Jobriath was multitalented—he wrote a symphony while still in high school—and certainly courageous. Truth be told, his material was a trifle naff. But his main issue was one of timing: glam had peaked, so the whole notion of Bowie 2.0 was met with derision. And then there was the gay thing. Jobriath showed the world what happens when you say you are gay *and you are not teasing*. His stated sexuality was a deal breaker. Danny Fields describes him as follows: "He was a talented songwriter but became the victim of overdone hype. It turned him into a joke before he really had a chance." Sadly he died of AIDS before he could give fame another shot.

Back in the day, Hollywood solved the problem by repackaging their gay stars as wholesome straight boys and providing them with "beards." Tab Hunter, Anthony Perkins, and Rock Hudson—closeted beauties of the '50s and '60s—were sent on paparazzi-friendly dates with eligible starlets. Pop music, like soccer, has struggled long and hard to figure out what to do with LGBTQ+ performers. Glam rock, so full of promise for unconventional outsiders, was ultimately more about showbiz flash for the straights than liberation for the gays. In fact, some gay liberationist factions were actively against the entire concept.

In issue 16 of *Come Together*, a British Gay Liberation Front magazine, a scribe named simply Geoffrey lets rip with a piece titled "Liberation via Eyeliner?" He states, "It is ironic that at a time when women are struggling to overthrow the cosmetic tyranny, many gay men are embracing it as potentially liberating, and super camps such as David Bowie are leading the campaign." According to the writer, gay men are sitting ducks for fads and trends as exemplified by "the fact that many people are willing to buy the most outrageous shoes with 3" to 6" heels," causing potential lifelong physical damage to foot and spine. Apparently gay men are being exploited by fashion promoters, "thereby perpetuating the myth of youth and that all gays 'die' at thirty." I bet Geoffrey was really fun at parties. I am sorry he never got to experience the life-affirming peacocking joy of showing off your glad rags and falling off your platforms on a Saturday night. As far as glam rock is concerned, *je ne regrette rien.* I would not have missed a single sequin of it.

And what about Lou?

I think it's fair to say that Lou had beaucoup glam rock regrets. His wife Bettye recalls the complex ways in which this phenomenon affected his career: "Glam rock was coming to America, and now, with *Transformer*, Lewis had been elected toastmaster." His retreat from glam rock was booze addled, anxious, and rapid. As Bettye recalls, "The problem with the Phantom of Rock persona is that it made him feel like a clown, which worked against him if he wanted his writing to be taken seriously."

For the rest of his career Lou studiously avoided frivolous theatricality. He was the opposite of Kiss.

Transgender superstar Holly Woodlawn in 1970. Two years earlier she
met Andy Warhol at the Factory and would enter his orbit.

(Jack Mitchell/Getty Images)

Drag Queens

It would be obscene, appalling, nay, downright rude to embark upon a dissection of the album *Transformer* (next chapter) without first chewing over the lives, personas, and significance of Holly, Jackie, and Candy.

Fifty years ago Lou Reed wove the names of three drag queens, Holly Woodlawn, Candy Darling, and Jackie Curtis, into his song "Walk on the Wild Side," tossing bouquets and Molotov cocktails far and wide. It was a brave choice, and hardly one that screams, "Casey Kasem is going to love this!" Casually and romantically riffing on the lives of these three badass trans bitches, in a way that romanticized and humanized them, was unprecedented, even by Lou's standards. Nobody could have predicted the strength of the reaction. In the ensuing decades the song has become the most listened to and parsed track in Lou's canon, and a historical benchmark for trans visibility and drag queens.

What is it about drag queens that galvanizes our attention? Why are they such objects of delight or, alternatively, disgust? Why have I personally frittered away so much of my life soaking up the ambience at drag venues, such as the Pyramid Club, L'Esqualita, Sally's Hideaway, the Plaza Salon, the Black Cap, Edelweiss, Wigstock, the Vauxhall Tavern, Susanne Bartsch's Copa, Bentley's, the Salon de Beauté, Jackie 60, and so many more, to mention nothing of fabulous dives in far-flung lands, the names of which have evaporated from my brain?

I'm not alone. Androgyny and transvestism have been enduring sources of fascination throughout history. Mythological deities, shamans, high priestesses, Shakespearean actors, music hall bawds, and cross-dressing carnies have been inspiring awe, repulsion, sexual attraction, fear, and loathing for thousands of years. Why? Yes, they are engaging and entertaining, but that fact alone does not explain the enduring power of the drag queen.

On *RuPaul's Drag Race* we observe the power of drag transformation amplified to a screeching decibel. These affable, creative lads arrive at work in the morning, clutching their lattes, looking cute and nonthreatening. Five hours, a pound of makeup, and a ton of wigs and costumery later, they are transformed into towering, seething termagants, ready to destroy. It's no accident that words like "slay" and "death drop," "gagging" and "killing," are part of the lingua franca of drag.

And what of the drag queen herself? Drag takes so much effort and commitment—if you have any doubts, try "tucking" with duct tape and get back to me—it is safe to assume that the motivations are many and various. They include gender expression, survival, masochism, sadism, revenge, a desire for attention. And money. Financial desperation and drag are intertwined, especially for drag queens of color. For most of history, drag has been defined as follows: women's clothing worn by a man for the purposes of entertainment—i.e., a paycheck. Drag is a power grab of the otherwise powerless. Drag is a money grab of the otherwise broke. This also applies to drag kings. But let's not get distracted. We are here to talk about Holly, Candy, and Jackie, three ladies who were no strangers to financial desperation.

Those girls wanted to be gawked at and desired and unconditionally worshipped and objectified and paid for and festooned with furs. Their certainty regarding their own movie-star beauty and gorgeousness—somewhat drug fueled—fascinated Warhol, who was delighted by their rabid self-belief. When Warhol said, "If you can convince yourself that you look fabulous, you can save yourself the trouble of primping," he must surely have been thinking of Holly and Jackie and Candy, lighting up the Factory with their confident charisma and insouciance.

In 1973 Holly Woodlawn gave us a window into daily life at the Factory when she was interviewed by *Lunch* magazine for their June issue. *Lunch* was billed as "the magazine for the new homosexual man and woman." "Can you describe a visit to the Factory?" asks the reporter, unleashing the kind of vivid, unfiltered response that only a drag queen can deliver: "Well, first of all you take the elevator, and when the elevator door opens on the sixth floor it says, KNOCK LOUDLY AND IDENTIFY YOURSELF. The door is locked. And then if Andy's there he's sitting behind his desk looking like the Wizard of Oz. And Paul's [Morrissey] in the other room talking on the phone, or maybe somebody's interviewing them. And you just sit around and you're made to feel dumb. Like you have to be a Maharajah to get noticed. That's the whole thing. If you were Mick Jagger they would give you a chair in a hot second and it'd be, 'Oh, Bianca, you must do this film ngngngngngn.' And when you walk in you're paranoid because they're taping everybody all the time, always with the tape recorders and the videotapes. Constantly. So I just have to go and get drunk and run up there and make this terrible noise . . . Oh, please. I should love to see some of the tapes they have of me! The last time I was there they called the police on me."

The Factory had three different locations between 1962 and 1984. The Silver Factory, so named because of the foil décor, lasted from '62 to '67 and was located on 47th Street. The rent was a hundred dollars per year. The focal point was a red couch, which Factory mainstay Billy Name had found on the street, and was featured in many photos and movies, most notably *Couch* and *Blow Job*. In '67 Warhol moved to the Decker Building on Union Square West. Business was booming. To maintain his output he acquired a significant retinue of workers, collaborators, and—drumroll!—drag queens. Warhol had a rigorous work ethic—there's a reason he named his studio the Factory—and regularly badgered the denizens of the Factory about their levels of productivity. Andy would ask Lou how many songs he had written on a particular day. Regardless of the answer, Warhol would reply, "You should do more." Yes, Warhol comes up relentlessly in this book, but keep in mind that, in addition to being a transpositive landmark, *Transformer* is Lou and Bowie's love letter to Andy and his world.

Bowie grew up in South London, far from Union Square and the madding crowds of Manhattan, at a time when drag was a frequent comedic trope. We British kids of the postwar era were literally drowning in drag. Every time you turned on the telly or went to a Christmas panto or a pub you encountered some dude with balloons stuffed down the front of his frock doing a highly misogynistic imitation of a feminine archetype, most likely his wife or mother. The most famous TV comedians of the '60s—Stanley Baxter, Dick Emery, Frankie Howard, Benny Hill, et al.—were straight guys who regularly dragged up on their weekly shows. The glamorous Danny La Rue—a combo of glamour drag and comedy drag—was a household name, performing before crowned heads. The all-male cast of Monty Python consistently portrayed angry menopausal women. Drag was bawdy, it was comedic, it was often sexist, and it was everywhere.

This was not the case in the US. While Bowie was being bombarded with drag over in Blighty, Lou was coming of age in a veritable drag desert. The guardians of morality were on high alert for commies and fags. Drag queens? Euch! The puritanical spirit of the US peaked in the 1950s, and the gendered clothing laws gave a green light to harassment.

The birth of anti-cross-dressing laws—an immensely complex subject with inconsistently enforced decrees varying state by state and going back two centuries—stemmed from an increase in dragtastic entertainment offered to the male-heavy frontier populations of settlers and prospectors. Think my friend Biddie, but a couple of centuries earlier. Over time these messy laws conflated cross-dressing with indecency and prostitution, further complicating the legal situation, but allowing for police harassment. Things got even more byzantine when, in the early twentieth century, women began to wear pants. Like I said, it's a knotty subject. The good news: post-Stonewall, cross-dressing arrests decreased. My point? When it comes to drag, the US had barely scratched the surface, while the UK had been tucking and frocking for millennia.

Every once in a while conventional establishment entertainers like Bing Crosby, Milton Berle, and Bob Hope would surprise their midcentury audiences—I'm imagining the Reeds huddled *en famille* in front of the TV in Freeport—by throwing on a frock for a cheap laugh, but you had to wait until the '70s, for a mainstream TV character like Flip Wilson's Geraldine. Flip's show became a cultural touchstone, and his catchphrases—"When you're hot, you're hot; when you're not, you're not," "The devil made me do it," and "What you see is what you get"—slipped into the national vocab.

When Lou encounters drag queens in person, it's in New York, in the margins of society, on the street, in the gay bars, in the gutter, and at the Factory, and it's never not transgressive, clandestine, taboo, and fun. In the Factory, where groovy monosyllabic folks are cool to the point of tedium, three glamorous, unpretentious goddesses like Holly, Candy, and Jackie create chaos, but they also provide a welcome relief.

Warhol loved to entice uptown society girls like Edie Sedgwick and Baby Jane Holzer into his world. Once he started making movies, he saw the need to add a little *je ne sais quoi* to the mix. "For a while we were casting a lot of drag queens in our movies because the real girls we knew couldn't seem to get excited about anything, and the drag queens could get excited about anything," remarks Andy in 1975 in *The Philosophy of Andy Warhol (From A to B and Back Again)*. With typical detachment, Warhol sidesteps the more complex fascinations with drag queens and tells us that they are, first and foremost, excitable. They deliver. They give value. Work-obsessed Warhol also has a profound respect for the commitment and effort required, stating, "I am fascinated by boys who spend their lives trying to be complete girls, because they have to work so hard—double-time—getting rid of the tell-tale male signs and drawing in all the female signs."

Warhol's *Flesh*, directed by Paul Morrissey, opens at the British Film Institute in 1970. A big censorship kerfuffle causes a publicity ripple, which reaches my ears, along with tidbits about blow jobs and drag queens. In 1970 I hitchhike across the UK (about forty miles) to the British Film Institute in London to see this movie. I am mesmerized by Joe Dallesandro's studly sensuality, but the money shot is delivered by Candy Darling and Jackie Curtis. It's love at first sight. Like many Warhol movies, *Flesh* manages to be simultaneously riveting and also an endurance test. (Remember, Warhol's stated goal of wanting to leave us "wanting less"?) The rivets are provided, in abundance, by these two drag queens.

The killer scene occurs when Candy and Jackie, sitting on a couch, peruse old Hollywood fan magazines and chat, like a couple of girls waiting at the nail salon, while Joe gets a noisy off-camera blow job from an exuberant cis lady of color named Gerri Miller. After complaining about her hairdresser—"Do you believe this hairdo cost ten dollars? TEN DOLL*EURS*? Andre did it. Andre of Paris on Fifth Avenue. I'm going to kill that queen Andre"—Candy compliments Gerri on her natural breasts, stating, "I think things that move are beautiful, like your bust. It moves." I am blown away by Candy. She is subtly and brilliantly hilarious.

Candy Darling was born two years after Lou, also on Long Island.* She is more the glamorous trans woman than a drag queen

---

* Candy's birth name was omitted, while Jackie's and Holly's birth dates and their original names were included. During her lifetime Holly, in particular, was very interested in talking about her origins and freely shared this information, rattling off her lengthy given name with relish and Puerto Rican pride. Jackie proudly proclaimed her East Village roots throughout her life. Candy, ever

per se. In the past there was a clear distinction between drag queens and those who had undergone full gender-reassignment surgery. In the UK bars of my youth—I'm thinking in particular of the Picador and the Rembrandt in Manchester—the trans women were often openly disdainful of those who had not yet transitioned, calling them "dress-ups."

Today all the old distinctions have dissolved. We are living in a freewheeling drag utopia where preconceived notions have been obliterated. Propelled by the onslaught of social media, drag is now a language that can be spoken in any context and by any person. A trans man like Gottmik can develop a full-blown drag identity and compete on *RuPaul's Drag Race*. Cis-gendered women might also drag up at weekends, or whenever they wish.

Back to Candy.

It's not uncommon for drag queens to worship a Hollywood star or two, but Candy's silver-screen fixation is unmatched. An obsession with movie-star glamour, with all its shimmering perfection, consumed her from an early age and informs her approach to drag. She is, to put it mildly, movie star identified. Her transition took her directly from grim boyhood—a violent drunken dad + bullying schoolmates—to Hollywood movie star, female. That prior life was her Norma Jean, and Candy is her Marilyn. As far as Candy is concerned the studio system still exists and Andy is her Louis B. Mayer.

In 1973 Candy interviews Lauren Hutton for Warhol's *Interview* magazine. At one point Hutton denies being a movie star,

the Hollywood star, was less inclined to publicly elaborate on the details of her painful childhood.

happily relinquishing that title to Candy: "No matter what I do in acting, whether I'm good, how much work I get, whatever, I will never be a movie star. Because I never will think of myself as one. You are a movie star because you think of yourself as a movie star and always have."

Hilton Als concurs. In an essay published in the catalog for the 1998 Whitney exhibit titled *The Warhol Look*—I was the installation designer—Als states the following: "Candy Darling's intense movie love, movie interest, was an outgrowth of her love for those actresses whose overbearing theatrical expressiveness in the films they made in the forties and fifties (and that Candy saw as a child on TV, on the *Million Dollar Movie*) transformed their star vehicles into epics. Candy Darling believed until the end in a Candy Darling epic being produced for her."

In *Flesh* we see how Candy combines movie-star charisma with a defiant Hollywood perfection. In her scene with Jackie Curtis, the tacky showbiz glam of the typical drag queen is clearly absent. In its place we see the Yves Saint Laurent 1971 look, complete with tie-neck blouse and smokey eyes and Carole Lombard hair. Candy's beauty and her faux/real movie-star sincerity give her a brittle allure. Whip-dancing Gerard Malanga describes her as follows: "There was nothing fragile about Candy. She was just a very potent, very powerful, very confident presence." A beturbaned Candy—Norma Shearer? Norma Desmond?—appears at her most confident, alongside Holly and Jackie, in *Women in Revolt* (1971).

Titled *My Face for the World to See*, Candy's journal was published in 1997 and contained photos, drawings, and many touching disclosures, including the following: "Someday I'll be a movie star. That's it. And I'll be rich and famous and have all the friends I want." I purchased a copy of this little pink book and later gifted it to a colleague who had professed a love for Candy. At the time of writing, this small book trades on Amazon for two thousand dollars. Half a century after her death Candy still has the following of a true movie star. There's no doubt that Lou's song "Walk on the Wild Side" aided and abetted her poignant quest for transcendent stardom, etching her memory into the culture.

Andy said, "Jackie Curtis is not a drag queen. Jackie is an artist. A pioneer without a frontier." Jackie Curtis was born John Holder Curtis Jr. in 1947 in New York City, and mostly raised by Grandma Slugger Ann, a notorious East Village bar owner.

In the movie *Women in Revolt*, Candy's chic glamour finds the perfect foil in Jackie Curtis, the uncrowned queen of hag drag. Or is it slag drag, or maybe drag-bag drag? Jackie's drag style is what my mother would have described as "hastily assembled," a slapdash street glamour of torn fishnets and disintegrating 1930s dresses—purloined from the closet of Slugger Ann, a former taxi dancer, that is to say a gal who danced with dudes for a nominal fee—and held together with safety pins. Her style has been much copied over the years. Stylists on *Vogue* photo shoots swipe images of Jackie's dégagé style for inspiration. Jackie's look has become wildly contemporary. Her finger-dabbed glitter makeup is a clear precursor of that worn by Rue, Zendaya's character in the hit series *Euphoria*.

Jackie's ramshackle appearance is deceptive. Of the three ladies under discussion, Jackie is by far the most accomplished. Danny Fields remembers her as "a great star and very smart. I remember first meeting her. She was an aspiring and perspiring teenager who had written a play." Poet and playwright, Jackie wrote and acted in various drag extravaganzas, including a play called *Glamour, Glory, and Gold*. In 1974, *Village Voice* reviewer Michael Smith describes this production as follows: "Its story of Nola Noonan, hash slinger to stripper to star to pitiful has-been, is a time-worn cliché out front, as well as a projection of the very fantasies Jackie, Candy, and other sex-switching pop show people have made their lives on for the past few years; but it is a second-hand rose of a fantasy in the first place, half mockingly contrived from careers that were themselves contrived by the star system and the economics of sexual frustration. So the play is half mocking about itself even while it is itself, while the publicity for it says Jackie Curtis *is* Nola Noonan. You don't know how to take him, her, or it. It is these ambiguities, and his spirit, that give the work its character and interest."

Ambiguity was Jackie's middle name. As is noted in Lou's song, Jackie alternated her drag persona with James Dean boy drag, stating, "I wanted to play James Dean, so I became him." Lily Tomlin recalled Jackie's fluidity in the documentary *Superstar in a Housedress* as follows: "You never knew how Jackie was gonna show up . . . you sort of envied someone who was so casually able to cross that barrier back and forth."

Jackie was a true rebel who defied categorization, literally, "I'm not a boy, not a girl, not a faggot, not a drag queen, not a transsexual—I'm just me, Jackie."

To appreciate Jackie's daring and impact, the reader may wish to enjoy her sizzling appearance in the counterculture documentary *WR: Mysteries of the Organism*. Watching Jackie sashay down 42nd Street through the hordes of pervs and tourists, towering over her petite male escort, slurping an ice cream, and startling the passing crowd with her defiant androgyny, is a real treat.

If Candy was a droll glamour-puss who worshipped cinema starlets like Kim Novak and Lana Turner, and Jackie was an accomplished enigma in a torn '30s tea dress, then Holly was a hurricane, which is apropos in a corny way since she originally hailed from Puerto Rico.

Holly Woodlawn, she of the plucked eyebrows and shaved legs, was born Haroldo Santiago Franceschi Ródriguez Danhakl in 1946 in Puerto Rico, and grew up in Miami. Then, as per the song, she fled, hitchhiking *her way across the USA*. "At the age of sixteen, when most kids were cramming for trigonometry exams, I was turning tricks, living off the streets, and wondering when my next meal was coming," recalls Holly in her knockabout autobio *A Low Life in High Heels*.

Holly's life was a farcical series of dragscapades, as exemplified by the fact that on one occasion she ended up in the New York Women's House of Detention, charged with attempting to impersonate the wife of the French ambassador to the United Nations. She was booted over to a men's facility when her secret was revealed.

Andy Warhol discovered Holly in Jackie Curtis's play *Glamour, Glory, and Gold*. Warhol movie director Paul Morrissey cast her in the film *Trash* and later in *Women in Revolt*. Her Warhol moment brought her stardom. "I felt like Elizabeth Taylor," Ms. Woodlawn told *The Guardian* in 2007, recalling her heyday as follows: "Little did I realize that not only would there be no money, but that your star would flicker for two seconds and that was it. But it was worth it, the drugs, the parties; it was fabulous."

While Candy is calm and Jackie is quizzical, Holly vibrates with manic, drug-fueled conviction. Every performance is a stomping tour de force of feminine self-belief.

For somebody who is so audacious, she has an instinctive understanding of the comedy that can be generated by dialing back the mania and playing it straight. In *Trash* she tells the social worker, "As you can see, I'm pregnant," while proudly stroking her obviously fake baby bump. In *Women in Revolt*, also produced by Warhol and directed by Paul Morrissey, Holly enthusiastically embraces the Women's Liberation Movement, despite later confessing that, in real life, she was totally unaware of it. Ms. Woodlawn plays a sex-crazed fashion model who claims to detest men and, along with Jackie and Candy, forms the militant organization named Politically Involved Girls, P.I.G. for short.

And Sugar Plum Fairy? Joe Campbell was not a drag queen per se. He was an actor who appeared in a Warhol movie titled *My Hustler*, playing an older hustler, named Sugar Plum Fairy. He was given this nickname by Dorothy Dean, a fascinating African American woman—a self-described "white faggot in a black woman's body" who also appears in *My Hustler*. Hilton Als's essay about Dottie titled "Friends of Dorothy Dean" is included in his book *The Women*, a brilliant personal exploration of race and sexuality identity.

Sugar Plum Fairy's inclusion in the song is the most random. While Little Joe Dallesandro was high up in the Warhol pantheon, a miracle of male objectification, Sugar Plum Fairy was a peripheral character. He nonetheless had an interesting life. He was in a relationship with gay activist icon Harvey Milk from 1955 to 1962. Another fun fact: In the 1960s he dated a guy named Oliver Sipple, who later made headlines when he, a heroic bystander, grabbed the gun away from would-be Gerald Ford assassin Sara Jane Moore, thereby saving the sitting president's life. But let's not stray any further off topic. We are here to underscore the majesty of Candy, Holly, and Jackie, the most famous trans personae of any popular song in history.

As you have probably gathered, the trans women—unlike the earnest Politically Involved Girls they play in the movie *Women in Revolt*—were not politically active in the conventional sense. Far from it. They were too busy trying to meet their own basic needs—with varying degrees of success—to spend time marching and handing out flyers. But there is no doubt that their lives, by their very nature, constituted bold political acts. And their presence on the cultural landscape—for my generation they were drag icons—provided gasoline for much of the political activity that would follow. "Walk on the Wild Side" became the inspirational soundtrack for many of the subsequent radical drag movements of the '70s, such as, for example, the Radical Faeries and the Sisters of Perpetual Indulgence. The bravado, humor, and theatricality of Andy's girls can be seen in both of these eccentric movements.

The Radical Faeries were founded in the late '70s in California. This particular group of activists extracted many values of the hippie counterculture from the previous decade, including paganism, communal living, free love, and nudity, and ran with them, far into the woods. The Radical Faeries enjoy skipping through nature and adorning themselves with body paint. They are the polar opposite of today's assimilation gays with their kids and mortgages.

The Sisters of Perpetual Indulgence are (still) equally and fabulously demented. Drag has always been an easy target for religious intolerance. The Sisters of Perpetual Indulgence began in 1979 as a spontaneous activist response to preachers who had begun to descend on the gay Castro area preaching hellfire and damnation to the LGBTQ+ community. With Warholian panache, a group of gays donned Belgian nuns' habits and gobs of *Rocky Horror* makeup and confronted the proselytizers, *et voilà*! A movement was born.

Lou's song is, was, and will always be a monumental hymn to a broad range of trans visibility. "Walk on the Wild Side," with its consistent presence on the airwaves, has become over time the pied piper of drag anthems, leading not just political messaging but also a delightful parade of entertaining individuals, which includes Sylvester, Jayne County, Bloolips, Boy George, Marilyn, Pete Burns of Dead or Alive, Divine, Tabboo!!, Lady Bunny, Lady Miss Kier, Flotilla Debarge, Lypsinka, Murray Hill, RuPaul, Alaska, Big Freedia, Trixie Mattel, Bob the Drag Queen, Linda Simpson, Trinity the Tuck, Sasha Velour, Silky Nutmeg Ganache, and, and, and . . . drag queens as far as the eye can see.

Lou Reed performing live in his customized velvet ensemble from Granny Takes a Trip. A Mick Rock photo from this same show became the *Transformer* cover.

(Mick Rock, 1972, 2022)

CHAPTER 6

The Album

It's the summer of '72, and the creation of *Transformer* at Trident Studios in London's seedy Soho, starring Reed, Bowie, and Ronson, is about to kick off. So what happens when these three glamorous varmints are flung into the collaborative hothouse of the recording studio for two weeks?

Of note are the respective ages of these three feral superfreaks. Bowie is twenty-five. Mick Ronson, aka Ronno, is one year older. These two blokes have barely reached the age when that lumpy bit on the brain has grown that controls judgment and impulse. Though I subsequently became a real Goody Two-Shoes, I myself was busted for reckless driving at the age of twenty-five and was also prone to telling people that I was going to move to Paris and live on the Rive Gauche and sell my body to older men. My point being that Bowie and Ronno are young and wicked.

Lou, at thirty, is the granddaddy of the group. In some ways he has seen so much; in others he is suffering from the arrested development that afflicts so many rock stars. Bowie, the youngest, appears to be the most evolved of the three.

I could lie and tell you that this was an explosive, apocalyptic collision of musical genii—Mozart, Beethoven, and Wagner—producing breakthroughs and epiphanies galore.

Or I could tell you it was like the three witches in *Macbeth*, each hag tossing all manner of musical toads and newts into a roiling cauldron, day after day, colluding on wicked spells and producing mysterious sounds and a new musical goulash that had never been tasted before. The reality is a little more mundane, though certainly not without interest or piquancy.

The earth-shattering, unconventional part of the whole enterprise was the decision to create an album for the LGBTQ+ audience. (They "thought it was dreary for gay people to have to listen to straight people's love songs.") Add to this the astonishing concept of marrying Lou's poetry with Bowie's production vision, and—bonjour!—how could *Transformer* ever not have been an interesting album? Lou's poetry—as per Danny Fields, "the greatest songwriter of his generation"—merges with the explosive new cult of Bowie-dom.

In a Classic Albums documentary on the album, Lou recalled the process as straightforward: "I just ran over the songs with them. By that, I mean the chord structure and the melody." In his memoir, *Abbey Road to Ziggy Stardust*, engineer Ken Scott—he functioned more like a producer—recalls the system used to lay down the tracks as follows: "Lou would teach Ronno the song, then Ronno would teach the session musicians, then we would carry on as if it were a Bowie record until it was time to do Lou's vocals."

With *The Man Who Sold the World*, *Hunky Dory*, and *Ziggy* under their belts, Bowie's team had developed a style, a formula, a winning schtick. Add Lou's lyrics, plus the inventive magic of musicians like bassist and tuba player Herbie Flowers and drummer John Halsey, and you have a solid foundation.

Ken Scott is one of a small group of survivors who have retained clear recollections of the recording sessions. Klaus

Voormann is another.* He plays bass guitar on "Perfect Day," "Goodnight Ladies," "Satellite of Love," and "Make Up," and has described the Trident fortnight in Scott's memoir as follows: "Lou and David got on like the world on fire. Those were two that found each other. Their discussions were witty, funny, and cheeky. Very camp, it was. Lou had his fingernails painted black. He played a fantastic rhythm guitar."

Very camp, it was. Hold that thought.

Bowie recalled in the documentary *Rock and Roll Heart* treading carefully around his elder, stating how he "felt so intimidated by my knowledge of the work he'd already done." Lou recalled a spirit of cooperation, and the pleasure of collaboration. He later stated, "[RCA] said, 'The first record was a flop, so go make another one.' You know, in those days they gave you a chance, you could go make another one. With Ronno and David there was a real simpatico, which is certainly part of the situation I had in the Velvets and it was miles above where I'd been on the *Lou Reed* record where there was nothing simpatico."

It wasn't all chuckles. The sessions were not without a few rock-star hissy fits, at least according to Angie Bowie, who remembers

---

* Klaus is a renaissance dude and a noteworthy figure in the music business. He played bass with Manfred Mann and is most noted for his later collabs with various former Beatles. (He was the roommate of Ringo and George in Hamburg.) He also designed the cover of the '66 Beatles album *Revolver* with its Beardsley-inspired line drawings and photo collage. Even at the age of twenty-five, Bowie is a magnet for interesting creatives.

Lou wigging out at Bowie and Ronno to such an extent that she fled the studio and "went shoe-shopping on Carnaby Street for an hour or two." Just another day at the office. There is no way to verify the content of the contretemps. It's probably just as well. It could easily have been something embarrassingly trivial: "Who the fuck put their cig out in my cuppa?"

Journalist Nick Kent recalls to author Dylan Jones the somewhat neurotic symbiosis that held the project together as follows: "Lou Reed viewed Bowie as Bette Davis viewed Eve in *All About Eve*. Lou Reed even referred to Bowie as Eve on several occasions. But once they worked together he realized Bowie had skills that he didn't have. The thing is, Bowie got Lou hits, he got Iggy hits. Up until Bowie they hadn't had any hits." Kent is alluding to the brilliant 1950 movie in which a fresh-faced young fan named Eve Harrington weevils her way into the life of an older megastar named Margo Channing and begins to devour the host. In Lou's analogy, he is Margo and Bowie is evil Eve.

So, with the clock ticking, they laugh and drink and swear at each other and then laugh again, and Ronno teaches the songs and Bowie adds his flourishes and Lou lays down his vocals, and Herbie Flowers does his marvelous thing and Ken Scott makes sure Lou's record sounds like a Bowie record, and out pops *Transformer*. Everyone works regular office hours to allow Ronno and Bowie to rehearse in the evenings for upcoming shows. It is all remarkably unremarkable. A bunch of creative dudes doing their jobs. No madness. No miraculous midnight epiphanies. Other than Lou's freak-out, there is minimal hysteria.

The real madness kicks off in November of that same year when *Transformer* is launched. The maniacs are the civilians, the public, the record buyers, me. The glamour, shlock, and awe of *Transformer* occurs once we, the fans, buy the record, plonk it on the turntable, start hitting each other with flowers, going totally fucking nuts and telling all our pals to buy the bitch. BUY IT NOW!

Fuck the critics, the managers, and the record companies and *Rolling Stone* and all the press, the marketing departments and the pundits. The music establishment and the press have always been treated like deities. Time for a revolution. The miracle of this album belongs to us, the lumpen masses who plonk down our hard-earned shekels, because we have no reservations. WE LOVE *Transformer* TO BITS.

We love it because not only is it original, funny, swinging, acidic, stupid, poignant, sentimental, ridiculous, and utterly brilliant, but we also dig this album because it is thoroughly enjoyable. Unlike some of the more dour offerings of the Velvet Underground, it requires no endurance, and no knowledge of the work of John Cage or Delmore Schwartz. We are left wanting more, not less. And not only is *Transformer* enjoyable; it is also enjoyably camp. And Lou's poetic songs have never been tighter and clearer and more genius. If this all sounds like I am having some kind of gay fit, then it's probably because I am. Ladies and gents and all those in between, let me refer you to Susan Sontag's "Notes on 'Camp,'" specifically numbers 55 and 56:

> 55. *Camp taste is, above all, a mode of enjoyment, of appreciation—not judgment. Camp is generous. . . . It only seems like malice, cynicism. (Or, if it is cynicism, it's not a ruthless but a sweet cynicism.) . . .*

> 56. . . . *People who share this sensibility are not laughing at the thing they label as "a camp," they're enjoying it.*

When I was a kid, a transformer was a sinister little thing—most likely yanked from a defunct radio or car—that we used to give each other electric shocks. (Not to be conflated in any way with Lou's shock treatment.) This was a very popular game in the 1950s. All you needed was a rudimentary electrical transformer, a flashlight battery, some wire, and a little group of scabby-kneed thrill seekers—standing in a circle on a school playground or a World War II bomb site—holding hands, waiting for the moment when the battery power was amped up by coiled wires inside the transformer, producing an electric shock and a collective squeal. *Collective Squeal* might have been a good title for *Transformer*, given how well it was received, and by whom.

The title *Transformer* checks many boxes. Transformation speaks to the process that we gay and trans people go through to find and reveal ourselves. It is also a nod to the repackaging process that is inherent in becoming a rock star. The notion of transformation is a leitmotif in the life and work of Andy Warhol—remember the 1962 nose-job paintings titled *Before and After?*—whose presence haunts this album. The title also brands Lou, the creator, as an agent of change, a Transformer. I for one am transformed.

Half a century later I distinctly recall the visceral delight I experienced on tearing this album out of its cellophane wrapper, vibrating with pleasure at the sight of Lou, sans sunglasses, wearing more heavy black eyeshadow than the Ronettes. The overexposed image of Lou—a fortuitous mistake that occurred in photographer Mick Rock's darkroom—reeks of druggy decadence. The gold scalloped valance recalls the faded facade of a tawdry burlesque joint.

Mick Rock nailed the image when Lou was playing live, in 1972, at the former King's Cross Cinema, which has since become the Scala. Upon seeing the image "Lou said immediately that was the shot," recalled Rock in *The Guardian* in 2021.

In the cover image, Lou is wearing an outfit unearthed for him by Angie Bowie at the legendary King's Road boutique named Granny Takes a Trip, a favorite style emporium of Mick and Keith and all the dedicated followers of whatever the hell they were following. According to cultural critic Paul Gorman, the jacket was a black velvet bolero, a style also owned by Keith Moon. In an effort to add some couture glam rock panache to this garment, Granny's tailoring legend Freddie Hornik rushed Lou's bolero over to his skilled seamstress auntie—her name was Alice Jarrett—at her home in Ealing, West London. Alice stayed up into the wee hours, attaching those sparkling embellishments, to create this iconic outfit for Lou.

The back cover shots were taken by Karl Stoecker, who went on to shoot the first three Roxy Music covers. The girl is well-known fashion model Gala Mitchell—a favorite of designer Ossie Clarke—deceptively styled à la drag queen. In 1975, on that same Netherlands cassette tape made while Lou was hanging out with a friend, the tape on which he states his intention to give the gays the music they deserve, Lou takes credit for the photograph of the back-cover siren: "It's a real drag queen. I went out to Club 82 in the 220 [sic] and found the person. I took them back for eight hours, taping them, taking Polaroids, until I took the picture, that was that." As multitalented as Lou was he would have been incapable of spontaneously producing the kind of polished professional glamour shot that adorns the back cover. It makes perfect sense that Lou, in the context of *Transformer*, wanted his back-cover gal to appear like a drag queen. It is quite possible—and this might explain any subsequent confusion on his part—that one of his drag-queen Polaroids ended up providing the inspiration for the Gala Mitchell image, a scouting shot, as it were. It's good to keep in mind that being a rock star is a very complex gig, a constant tap-dancing performance, during which all the young dudes create their own legends. As a result they can tend to be unreliable narrators. Regardless, I would love to see Lou's gritty source material from his Club 82 shoot.

The back-cover dude is Lou's former road manager Ernie Thormahlen with a banana (inside a sock) stuffed down his pants. Ernie also worked for Mick Rock and played a role in art-directing the cover. *Sticky Fingers*, the Stones album with the cover designed by Andy Warhol and featuring the (real) zippered crotch of Little Joe Dallesandro, dropped the year prior, causing an erotic frisson. The *Transformer* back cover with its explicit hard-on image goes one step further. I am squinting in disbelief.

At the time of the release there is a widespread rumor that added an additional sizzle—Tim Blanks and I, at opposite ends of the Old Commonwealth, both heard it, and believed it. Tim recalls, "The rumor about the back cover of *Transformer* was that the girl and the guy were the same person, which fit with the whole idea of transformation."

As it turns out, I was able to talk to Karl Stoecker himself, who happily shed light on the back-cover Gala/Ernie shoot. It appears Karl and Lou had attended Syracuse at the same time, taken classes together, and become friends and creative collaborators. Karl was the roomie of Jim Tucker, brother of soon-to-be VU drummer Maureen. After college Karl visited Lou and John Cale in their downtown abode and recalls it as "the dirtiest apartment I had ever seen." He attended VU concerts including the Exploding Plastic Inevitable where he enjoyed the spectacle of his former roommate's sister using a garbage can in lieu of a drum. Karl moved to London and began shooting retro pin-up images of girls, forging the template for the famous Roxy Music album shoots. Karl and Lou reconnected when the former was hired to shoot the *Transformer* back-cover images. Karl recalls that he and Lou wanted the guy and gal to somehow mirror each other, gender-wise. A stud and a starlet. (Karl does not recall any talk of drag queens per se.) Gala would be the hyper-fem retro pin-up and Ernie would be the rough-trade dude, styled in the manner of the bulging boys depicted in Tom of Finland's homoerotic drawings. Ernie's infamous banana came from a bowl of plastic fruit that was lying around the studio.

Clearly one is in for a treat. Or is one? It's all very well loving the cover. But is the album any good?

Back in 1972 buying an edgy album like this was a bit of a crap-shoot. Velvet Underground albums and the like were never going to be played on the radio. Purchases were made based on loyalty to a particular artist. You would read about it in a rock mag and then, without having heard it, you would make the momentous decision to open your handbag. If you were lucky, you heard a chunk of it at a party or on a late-night radio show. You could also ask to listen to it in the record shop in a dopey pegboard booth or with headphones. But there was invariably a line of people waiting who would start tapping on the window and glaring, especially if you attempted to slog through an entire album.

Praying I have not wasted my dough, I plonk it on the turntable.

The moment Lou and the boys tear into "Vicious" my gay chakras start tingling.

This kick-off song sets the tarty, bitch-slapping tone for the whole album. It is dance-y, funny, light, and heavily scented with the presence of Bowie and Mick Ronson. The introspective poetic doom of the Velvet Underground is dialed back. Lou's poetry sparkles in the sunlight. It feels right for the moment. Life is grungy enough in 1972. Time to shimmy. "Vicious" is more like a sunny Saturday on trendy King's Road, a runway of fashion exhibitionism, than a drug comedown at the Factory.

What makes "Vicious" sound gay? The hyperbole of the title is pure camp. Walter Cronkite or Howard Cosell—archetypes of mainstream straight-guy parlance back then—would only resort to using the word "vicious" in the context of objective brutality, such as a sectarian war or a vindictive football tackle. Whereas we gays take words like "vicious," "wicked," and "evil" and apply them to minor interpersonal infractions or even inanimate stuff, like a cheap cologne or a set of offensive curtains. Such is the nature of camp. Example: Bloke A emerges from his boudoir wearing a new green sweater. Bloke B says, "When did you decide that green was *your* color?" Bloke A replies, deadpan, "No need to be vicious." Exaggeration is our reality. Overstatement is our oxygen.

Another gay giveaway: the fact that the protagonist and the "you" in the song are both hitting each other with flowers and sticks and stepping on each other's hands and feet calls to mind the relentlessly bitchy queens in *The Boys in the Band*. The Mart Crowley blockbuster play about a gay birthday party opened in '68 and the brilliant movie directed by William "The Exorcist" Friedkin hit the screens in 1970, making big cultural waves and forever linking homosexuals—New York gays in particular—with unhinged, drunken, catty behavior.

When I first catch the lyrics—Lou's diction throughout is crystal clear, no whispering or mumbling—I assume these are nutty rhymes written by Lou in the spirit of Delmore Schwartz, but also *Alice's Adventures in Wonderland* or possibly Edward Lear's *Book of Nonsense*. I surrender to the playful surrealism. During the course of researching for this book I read endless earnest speculative analysis. Lewis Carroll and Lewis Reed both knew how to let their imaginations take a trippy turn and paid this forward to their audience. My advice would be to luxuriate in the creative idiocy and not to try too hard to see patterns and meaning where none exist.

One is reminded of Truman Capote's description of Andy Warhol. Paraphrasing the title of an Oscar Wilde story, he dubbed Warhol "a sphynx without a secret." Some of Lou's songs are like "The Ostrich," the song he wrote and performed with the Primitives. They just sound good. There is less than meets the ear. Sometimes an ostrich is just an ostrich.

The "Vicious" flower reference has also been endlessly parsed, many seeing it as yet another dig at the hippie counterculture that is shriveling and retreating in the white-hot glare of glam rock. However, in 1989 Lou told *Rolling Stone*, "Andy said, 'Why don't you write a song called "Vicious"?' I said, 'Well, Andy, what kind of vicious?' 'Oh, you know, like I hit you with a flower.'" *Et voilà!* A perfect example of that Wilde-ian, Firbank-ian camp hyperbole.

To reiterate: Camp is a slippery bitch, hard to define, difficult to grasp, and resistant to logic. Don't beat yourself up if you are struggling a little. Camp is a shape-shifting apparition. This is the reason Sontag wrote a series of notes, rather than a formal essay.

The second track is titled "Andy's Chest." The playful lyrics, with their references to dentured ocelots and knights in flaming robes, remind me of the work of surrealist artist Leonora Carrington. As previously mentioned, "Andy's Chest" was written three years prior to the recording session, as a response to the '68 shooting of Andy Warhol by radical feminist Valerie Solanas, she of the Society for Cutting Up Men (S.C.U.M.). By the time *Transformer* hits my turntable, Valerie Solanas is back on the street, and phone-stalking Factory employees, having spent a mere three years in jail for the almost-murder of Andy.

The oblique, abstract nature of the lyrics might be explained as follows: given that Val was no longer incarcerated, an explicit song about the pain and suffering endured by Andy might well have made Lou her next target. The overall mood of the song is anxious, reflecting the Manson era. The subtext of this track is clear: Being groovy will not save you. Hip people get brutalized too, and in a literal way, not a camp way. The lyrics are, like so much of Lou's poetry, open to interpretation. A good pal of mine, a smart Lou watcher, contends that this track is very much a love song to Andy, and that Lou is basically promising his kingdom to his wounded mentor.

Speaking of love songs: Upon first hearing, I assume that "Perfect Day," the third track on *Transformer*, is a piss-take. The swirling romance of the musical arrangement calls to mind *Love Story*, the lines-around-the-block movie starring Ryan O'Neal and Ali Mac-Graw that opened a couple of years prior. The whole concept of a romantic New York montage—a young couple feeding animals, sipping sangria in the park, and then taking in a movie—is astonishingly twee and so jarringly dissonant with Lou's amphetamine, heroin, outlaw persona that surely there has to be some kind of twist. Maybe, at the end of this idealized date, a dead body shows up in the park, like in Antonioni's 1966 movie *Blow-Up*.

"Perfect Day" is actually a song Reed wrote after time spent with his first wife, Bettye, then fiancée. There exists a beautiful version in Lou's archives where the couple can be heard toying with an alternative chorus of "Just a summer's day." Bettye sings in her wavering falsetto while Lou plays waltz piano behind it.

The Velvet Underground had occasional forays into this kind of sweetness with songs like "Sunday Morning," but "Perfect Day" is in a class of its own, and with immense, broad, let's-play-it-at-our-wedding appeal. Mick Ronson's contribution cannot be underestimated. The working-class Yorkshireman, who, lest we forget, was best known at that moment for standing onstage while a kneeling Bowie fellated his guitar, revealed his musical talents by creating a veritable movie soundtrack of string arrangements that seduce even the more cynical listener into surrendering to "Perfect Day."

I would love to see an accounting balance sheet detailing how much money this song has made from commercial licensing in the intervening years. The universal beauty of the sentiments expressed by Lou have guaranteed the presence of "Perfect Day" in a broad spectrum of commercial contexts in the half-century since it was created.

In a weird way this is the bravest song on the album. The boys collectively leave their cynicism and their fear of not being cool at the door and create a beautiful track with mainstream sentimental appeal. And it's 100 percent inclusive. Lou's lyrics do not specify gender, allowing us gays to see ourselves, guzzling sangria and chucking nuts at the Central Park squirrels with the best of them.

And then the body in the park, the chilling denouement. The sweetness falls away as Lou laments the fact that he is not a good person. He then issues a blunt warning: Somebody—is it Bettye?—will reap what she has sewn. When Bettye first heard this chorus, she should probably have yelled, "Taxi!" (More on their relationship in a moment.)

I take no issue with throwing in a couple of fillers. Every album needs a lemon sorbet or two, and there is a general consensus that track 4, "Hangin' 'Round," falls into this category. It's a tight, swinging ditty that also serves to remind the listener this is a rock album. A filler track also gives those earnest musicologists a chance to sharpen their analytical skills and produce a speculative analysis of Lou's lyrics. Who are Harry, Jeanny, and Kathy, and what did Harry do with Dad's bod after he dug it up?

Prepare for a massive switching of gears.

Being well versed in the Warhol dramatis personae, I am riveted by track number 5, "Walk on the Wild Side," by far the most significant cut on *Transformer*.

"Walk" has as an interesting genesis: Lou was originally commissioned to write a song for a musical version of Nelson Algren's eponymous work. The original plot concerns the plight of Dove and Kitty, a boy and a girl, who hitchhike and train-hop their way south to New Orleans during the Great Depression and find themselves embroiled in a steamy world of bordello sleaze. The project fell through, and Lou rewrote the song, framing it to focus on the glamorous outsiders in the Warhol milieu, thereby making the song legendary.

I am immediately smitten. It's 1972. I am a gay bloke, listening to tales of drag queens, on an album I just bought in the Manchester town center. This is so fucking insane. I am just about ready to blow a gay gasket. As previously noted, gay gasket blowing was very much Lou's intention.

For his revised *Transformer* version of "Walk on the Wild Side" Lou Reed also took inspiration from Capucine, the beauteous one-namer whose cheekbones chew the scenery in the movie version of Algren's tale. Capucine's icy androgyny made her a gay icon. She possessed the same ambiguous beauty as Bowie, calling to mind the famous Sontag observation: "What is most beautiful in virile men is something feminine; what is most beautiful in feminine women is something masculine."

The opening credits of the movie *Walk on the Wild Side* are possibly the most astonishingly perfect in the history of cinema, and, in the absence of an official video for Lou's song, provide a great visual accompaniment. (Try it!) It's hard to imagine that the prowling cat, with his/her silky stride, was not part of the inspirational mix that guided Bowie and Lou and Ronno as they constructed their elegant, prowling mistresspiece.

At the core of this track is the electrifying juxtaposition between the sordid screenplay of Lou's poetry—the brave, beleaguered Holly, Candy, and Jackie, Little Joe and Sugar Plum, navigating the streets and the hostility of society—and the sumptuous musical arrangement. It's like a corpse in a satin-lined coffin. Every aspect of it, from the sliding Herbie Flowers bass to the chanting chorines with their *de-do-de-do*, provides the perfect foil for the gritty images that unfurl as you listen to the lyrics. The dissonance—luxury vs. gutter—is the everything of this track. The lives of the Warholites are elevated and made romantic in a way that is simultaneously camp but also deeply affecting. The soaring arc of the music shines a poignant eternal spotlight on Holly and the gang, in a way that a more grim, punked-out arrangement would not have succeeded in doing.

Any discussion of this track through the LGBTQ+ lens desperately needs a shout-out to Little Joe. Since Holly, Candy, and Jackie were given their due in the preceding "Drag Queens" chapter, let's give Joe a moment.

Joe Dallesandro was a Florida runaway who found his way to the Factory via nude modeling and homoerotic movies in which he sported his self-administered Little Joe tattoo. A small baroque scroll, bearing the word "Little," adorns his upper right arm. Directly underneath is the name "Joe." Joe and his tattoo star in *Flesh*, *Trash*, and *Heat*, underground Warhol-Morrissey movies that relentlessly objectify his youthful muscularity in a manner that is high camp and turns Joe Dallesandro into a gay icon. His perfect catlike features, his pin-straight hair, bandana and jeans, and his physique-magazine bod made him the most enduring sex symbol of underground movies. The poster for *Flesh*—a naked Joe playing with his naked kid—also became iconic.

In the mid-'80s I designed the set for a Mabou Mines play

titled *It's a Man's World*, written by Greg Mehrten. The lead character, played by Greg, was loosely based on Sal Mineo, the closeted gay actor who was murdered by a trick. I needed an evocative something-or-other for the main character's bedroom wall, a shorthand visual that would clearly identify him as a happening, late-'60s, gay-but-closeted actor, so I push-pinned Joe's *Flesh* movie poster to the wall. Cue the applause.

The "Walk" reference to "Little Joe" refers to his tattoo and not to other parts of his body, if you get my drift. Joe was not entirely pleased with his inclusion in the song. In 2014 he told the *LA Weekly*, "I didn't have any relationship with Lou back then. We hadn't met during that time. We never talked. What happened was Lou wanted to have his own career and get away from the Velvets. Paul [Morrissey] suggested he do a song about the people in the Factory and in his movies. So Lou watched *Flesh*. He saw some of the people at Max's Kansas City too. He sat down and wrote 'Walk on the Wild Side' about us. But it was the character he wrote about. Not me."

Joe is bisexual, has been married three times, and fathered three kids. In 2018 he told *Hero* magazine, "I always felt as I was growing up that my tattoo was the stupidest thing I ever did. They show forever, you can't be 'Little Joe' forever, and in movies they couldn't cover one that big with make-up." "Walk on the Wild Side," with its enduring appeal, shows that, for good or bad, you can be Little Joe forever.

On hearing the song, it is immediately obvious that this track is the set piece of *Transformer*. "Walk" has diverse musical contributions. Ken Scott recalls that Flowers came up with that magical opening bass after the track was laid down. Ronnie Ross, Bowie's saxophone teacher, played the baritone sax. Bowie's commitment to the sax was polarizing. This instrument was, for my generation, so associated with Glenn Miller and other '40s big bands that we relegated it to history, a mums-and-dads instrument. We deemed it quite naff. Bowie de-naffed the saxophone and single-handedly made it groovy again. Andy Mackay of Roxy Music also did his bit.

Thunderthighs, the backup singers, were brought in by Ken Scott to add the *do-de-do*s. He had worked with them previously. Dari Lalou, Karen Friedman, and Casey Synge were white and two of them were Jewish. Ken Scott recalls: "While the line of the song goes, 'And the colored girls say . . .' it's more like 'And the Jewish girls say . . .'" Regarding the use of the word "colored": This was considered an acceptable term in the '70s, as exemplified by the title of Ntozake Shange's award-winning play *For Colored Girls Who Have Considered Suicide/When the Rainbow Is Enuf.* When mores changed, so did Lou. When performing the song in later years, he switched the lyrics to "And the girls say . . ."

When the time came to do final mixes, Ken Scott recalls Bowie was on the *QE2* to the US due to his fear of flying. Ronno came by for one mix and Lou "was there physically but not mentally." Ken was starting to get a little sick of the repetitive nature of the *do-de-do*s so he had the girls try walking forward toward the mikes, until they were singing "right in your face." Good job, Ken.

This song is ultimately a hymn to visibility. In 1975 Lou recalled in that taped Rotterdam conversation with his friend, "It was so nice when this song came out. Candy said to me . . . I was at the Factory . . . I was afraid maybe some of them would be mad at me, but everybody liked it. They said, 'it's so nice to hear ourselves.'"

The first track on side 2 is titled "Make Up," and it is so deliciously swanky and gay-positive that, upon first hearing, I think I am going to plotz. Herbie Flowers's oompah tuba instantly calls to mind *Cabaret*, the movie that, the same year, permeates every aspect of the culture, dumping bisexuality, decadence, and transvestism on an even wider audience than *Transformer*. In a desperate attempt to achieve the prewar Weimar look, my pals and I start plastering down our hair with brilliantine to look like Michael York, using cigarette holders (again), and smoking colored Sobranie cocktail cigarettes. Girls cut their bangs into a point, as per Liza Minelli's character Fräulein Sally Bowles, and they paint their fingernails iridescent green. And so do some boys.

Regarding the lyrics: As I listen, I wonder if Lou is singing about his own new penchant for makeup. Is he alluding to his soon-to-be wife Bettye? If so, he is celebrating makeup in a way that would be atypical of the average straight dude, unless he happened to be a door-to-door Avon man. Maybe—just a thought—Lou is actually riffing on the Factory girls.

In addition to the drag queens, Warhol's Factory is replete with females, groovy chicks, society girls like Edie Sedgwick, Baby Jane Holzer, and Warhol superstars like Viva and Ultra Violet. These vamps and camps have many of the attributes of drag queens. The gay men in the Factory milieu are riveted by these reckless glamour girls in their Paco Rabanne dresses made from plastic discs and their obsession with their increasingly elaborate maquillage. Warhol gets lyrical about Susan Bottomly's beauty routine in his memoir *Popism*, describing how she would "spend hours putting on the latest makeup, stroking on Fabulash over and over again, painting her eyes three different shades of brown . . . Watching someone like Susan Bottomly, who had such perfect, full, fine features, doing all this on her face was like watching a beautiful statue painting itself."

This theory does not entirely explain the inclusion of the lines "now we're coming out, out of our closets," lyrics that instantly render this song the most overtly "out" track on the album. Yes, this was a moment when male pop stars and, one assumes, a fair number of their gay male fans might be giving the mascara brush a whirl, but the coming-out message, combined with all the Max Factor, boldly underscores the overall inclusivity of the album and, without question, yodels the drag queens back to center stage.

And who, pray, is the "slick little girl" in the chorus of "Make Up"? The most obvious candidate is Jane Forth, Joe Dallesandro's skeletal costar in the movie *Trash*. In 1970 the *New York Times* declared Jane Forth "the face of now," elaborating as follows: "In a city of unusual faces, Jane Forth stands out. Hers is a cadaverous face, a high fashion face, half Garbo, half moon child. The lips are bright red, the pale cheeks rouged. The eyebrows are shaved off until only the beginnings—looking like two apostrophes—remain. The dark hair is slicked back with Wesson Oil to form a tight bun at the nape of the neck." Her slickly Wessoned hair appears painted onto her scalp. To quote the Florence Henderson commercial for this product, Jane Forth has "Wessonality."

As I take in "Satellite of Love"—track 2, side 2—I am reminded that glam rock was nothing if not space oriented. Bowie's Spiders are, after all, from Mars. His breakthrough hit had been "Space Oddity." Everyone is wearing space boots. Something about glam rock screams interplanetary glamour. When Oasis have their '90s hit "Champagne Supernova," I think of "Satellite of Love." The words don't make much sense in either song, but both offer the listener an intergalactic whoosh of rocket-ship positivity. "If it was unearthly to be queer, then 'Starman' proved that the queer kids came from a world brighter than Earth," notes Sasha Geffen in her book *Glitter Up the Dark*, adding, "Bowie cast his transgression not as a failure of masculinity but as a transcendence of masculinity, of joyous belonging to a celestial world beyond our own."

As with "Walk on the Wild Side," the magic of this track comes from dissonance. With "Walk" it is the chasm between the lives of the reviled outsiders and the soaring production. In the case of "Satellite of Love," it's the baroque doo-wop production juxtaposed with the deadpan, downbeat subtlety of Lou's delivery. He really does sound like a beaten-down voyeur, a guy who prefers to "watch things on TV" or passively observe the person who is being so "bold with Harry, Mark, and John." All the while the romantic tinkling piano and Bowie's rococo *pom, pom, pom* vocals provide the perfect foil. "David's amazing at background vocal parts—*bom, bom, bom*—that's okay, that's really great, but the really great thing is the high note at the end," Reed would later marvel in the Classic Albums documentary. "Very few people could do that. I just loved when he did that, I mean—what a move. When he goes up like that . . . really pure and beautiful." As with "Andy's Chest," "Satellite of Love" was a previously recorded VU song that was slowed down and reimagined for *Transformer*.

Lou is a guy who often struggled to get out of his own way. One wonders how he (Margo) reacted when Bowie (Eve) began throwing down those soaring *pom, pom, pom* falsetto background vocals. (Maybe this was the cause of the eruption that saw Lou going postal and Angie fleeing for retail therapy.) How did Bowie talk taciturn Lou into acquiescing to his brilliant flights of fancy? This speaks to the electricity and charisma that emanated from Bowie at this particular moment.

Lou remains satellite-obsessed. In that '75 Rotterdam cassette-recorded conversation he announces, "Some people don't know that they are satellites," an ambiguous comment that leaves one wondering, *Is it good or bad to be a satellite?*

Along with "Hangin' 'Round," "Wagon Wheel," though enjoyable, is definitely filler. The trigger warning comes right at the beginning, when Bowie and Ronno, possibly unsure of what else to do, let rip with a falsetto, "Spoke . . . Spoke." Geddit? Wheel, spoke?

Struggling to find a more profound rationale for this song, I begin to wonder if Wagon Wheel was the name of a gay bar. In John Waters's 1974 movie *Female Trouble*, starring the late great Divine, a gay bar named the Wagon Wheel gets a hearty shout-out. Divine's rival, the terrifying Aunt Ida, played by Edith Massey, is desperately trying to turn her nephew gay. She describes heterosexuality as "sick and boring," begs to bleach his hair, and implores him to go to the Wagon Wheel and pick up a nice boy. Aunt Ida's transgressive advice got huge belly laughs in the movie theatre because it was the exact opposite of what was actually happening in the world. The scared-straight attitudes experienced by Lou and myself in the '50s and '60s persisted. Boys were being given reparative therapy and electric shock treatment into the 1970s and beyond.

I vividly remember a college field trip to a Gothic mental asylum on the outskirts of Manchester around the time of *Transformer*'s release. At one point in the tour, we psychology students were shown the darkened room where "aversive conditioning" therapy was administered to those wishing to be de-gayed. The patient sat in a chair and was shown images of attractive blond surfers and given a mild electric shock. The physician explained that the success of the treatment was determined using criteria for masculine and feminine behavior. This, the doc admitted, was not without its challenges since there were so few behaviors or traits that were exclusively masculine or feminine. The one reliable indicator he underscored, was the wearing of nail polish on the toes. Apparently, this was the one thing men NEVER did, the ultimate marker of masculinity. At this point the entire class pivoted and smirked in my direction. Some whooped. Too chickenshit to brave the streets of Manchester with electric-blue nail polish on my fingernails, I was wearing it covertly on my toes and had acquired a reputation for doing so among my housemates and pals.

Was I traumatized by this trip? For some reason, it left me oddly unmoved. It was all presented so matter-of-factly that I just accepted there were people who could not cope with being different, had no desire to bop down to the Wagon Wheel, and wished, for some unearthly reason, to join the "sick and boring" world of the heterosexual.

Next track: When I first hear it, I find "New York Telephone Conversation" to be wildly intoxicating, simply because I have no telephone and neither does anybody else in my orbit, other than my parents, and they share a party line with the folks across the street. My pals and I make plans when we see one another and tend to stick to them. If I desire to make a telephone call—this happens rarely and usually when something gnarly has occurred—I trudge to the red telephone booth two streets away and wait, often in the rain, until the previous caller vacates. The whole concept of yammering on the phone—in the comfort of your home!—seems so incredibly decadent and glamorous. Oh, to live in New York and while away the time bullshitting, possibly whilst still in bed, about the previous night's activities. Some of the UK success of *Transformer* can be attributed to the fact that it brought a whiff of New York szhooshiness to us Brits who were living through another wave of British austerity.

Any homage to Warhol would be remiss not to comment on his addiction to gossip and endless phone jabbering. According to Lou in the taped Rotterdam conversation with his friend, the intended targets of this satirical song—Andy? Brigid Berlin? Warhol business manager Fred Hughes?—got the message loud and clear and were incensed. Lou recalled, "This was a thing we did for one minute on purpose. It was aimed at a certain New York circle of people who knew who they were and were so offended by it that all hell broke. We were too big to be hurt."

Upon first hearing the next track, "I'm So Free," I immediately conclude that I must surely be listening to an homage to the Cream song "I Feel Free" from 1966. I have a special relationship with Eric, Ginger, and Jack. As a devoted fan of psychedelic rock, I entered a competition—as I recall, I simply had to send in a postcard with my name on it, which was then randomly extracted from a mailbag!—to win the *Best of Cream* album in 1969, AND I WON!! The album never arrived chez moi so, being the persistent little fan that I was, I sent follow-up nagging letters to the radio station. Finally it arrived, scratched and with the sleeve covered with coffee rings and cigarette ash. I was delirious. Clearly the DJ had sent me *his* copy! I now felt part of the groovy music scene. (They would probably have done anything to stem the tide of nagging letters.)

Bowie also loved this Cream song and did his own version later on the '93 album *Black Tie White Noise*, the title of which was doubtless inspired by the VU album *White Light/White Heat*. Inspiration is everywhere. Take it, grab it, make it your own. When I was a window dresser, my ideas were often copied. It always made me so happy. The only thing worse than being copied is not being copied.

During the recording sessions, Angie Bowie and David took Lou on pub crawls in Soho, near Trident Studios. Lou dug the sordid nonthreatening coziness of Soho bohemia, a nice break from the mean streets of Manhattan. When Lou heard the traditional pub closing-time calls—"Time, gentleman, please," "Goodnight, ladies"—did he get inspired to write "Goodnight Ladies," the last song on the album? Turns out that this ditty, along with "Perfect Day," was played live at Max's during Lou's 1970 summer residency there with the Velvet Underground. And the source of inspiration, though it involves pubs, was more complex, highbrow even.

There is a nod to English pub life in "Goodnight Ladies," but it comes via the end of the "A Game of Chess" section of T. S. Eliot's "The Waste Land," a poem that Lou admired. Eliot deftly collages closing-time pub speak with Ophelia's suicidal departure speech from Hamlet.

As Lou was wont to remind journalists on multiple occasions, he was, after all, an educated dude. In a BBC documentary titled *Lou Reed Remembered*, we see him reminding the interviewer not once but twice: "You should keep in mind I got a BA in English. I graduated college. I'm aware of irony and distance"; "I'm street with a BA in English." Though *Transformer* is not weighed down with intellectual profundities, it is the output of an educated person. It has layers. There is emotional gravitas. There is sadness and poignancy and depth, all made more effective by the juxtaposition with *Transformer*'s overall playfulness and frivolity.

Transformer is a tribute to Andy's world, and is infused, appropriately, with the detached, fey Warholian worldview. Warhol once said, "In some circles where very heavy people think they have very heavy brains, words like 'charming' and 'clever' and 'pretty' are all put-downs; all the lighter things in life, which are the most important things, are a put-down." *Transformer*, with its idiosyncrasy, charm, and lightness, is a fitting homage to Warhol. And Lou? He was cursed with a heavy brain.

In his quest for hits Lou allowed his poetry to be reframed in the glam rock vernacular by a guy who was five years his junior. When success came to him, he was sharing the reins. This is, of course, why Lou was always a little ambivalent about *Transformer*. Lou's Kafkaesque worldview prevents him from enjoying the lighter things in life. As we have seen, niceness in others brings out the worst in him. The lightness and campness and success of *Transformer* ultimately gave him pause rather than pleasure.

Lou's ambivalence about this album became legendary and appears to have kicked in before completion. As noted previously, Ken Scott describes Lou as checked-out during the final mixing process at Trident. Maybe he already sensed that this glittery summer was not going to provide a long-term career solution. Scott recalls that a couple of weeks after finishing *Transformer* he ran into Lou in a Chinese restaurant and Lou had no idea who he was. This same blanking happened again at a TV studio. Scott said, "Hi," and Lou responded with, "Who is this guy?'

In subsequent decades he was incapable of directing any full-blown enthusiasm or gratitude toward Bowie. Every compliment had a subtle edge. In Dylan Jones's *David Bowie: The Oral History*, Lou states about Bowie: "He's very good in the studio. In a manner of speaking he produced an album for me."

It's good not to overinterpret any bad-mouthing, badinage, or fisticuffs. The music biz is tough on relationships. As mega-manager Simon Napier-Bell so eloquently put it, "All artists are deadly rivals even when they're pretending not to be." Love and hate are close neighbors in the cutthroat male-dominated world of rock. It's like Mick and Keith. Boys get stroppy with each other then they make up. And then they get stroppy again. And when they seem all palsy-walsy, they are often masking massive hostility. If you, dear reader, are looking for a genuine heartwarming Lou-Bowie moment, then reread Klaus Voormann's observations of the two lads larking about in the studio, getting on "like a world on fire." This may well have been them at their closest.

Holly Woodlawn, Jane Forth, and Joe Dallesandro, the stars of Paul Morrissey's movie *Trash*, in 1970.

(*Jack Mitchell/Getty Images*)

CHAPTER 7

Reaction

I am just going to come right out and say it: the music business has always been a tad homophobic—confused, some might say. Heroic masculinity—the chest-beating macho guitar god offering salvation or damnation—is a central archetype of rock mythology. Rock has a discordant relationship with limp-wristed-ness, kink, bisexuality, homosexuality, and transvestism—you know, the fun stuff. Elvis was pilloried for wearing a gold lamé suit. Mick Jagger was slagged off for resembling an ugly girl. Pretending to be a bit femmy worked for the gay and female fans, but God forbid you actually *were* a friend of Dorothy. Little Richard, Elton John, Freddie Mercury all hid their proclivities to safeguard their careers. Indie darling Wayne/Jayne County is the only standout loud-and-proud trans rocker from Lou's generation.

It's a miracle that any LGBTQ+ individuals ever gave it a shot in the music business. A creative gay with half a brain knew instinctively that pop stardom was an unrealistic goal. Better to become a puppeteer.

During my youth, ambitious gay men who were drawn to the sizzle of the music business more often assumed string-pulling Svengali roles, with staggering results. In the 1960s young working-class lads were looking for ways to kick against the establishment. Join a band. Check! And then what? An image makeover, but supervised by whom? The young oiks were enabled in the pop-star transformation process by an entire cabal of cultivated, eccentric, bossy, overachieving, influential homosexuals, dubbed "the Velvet Mafia" by Darryl W. Bullock in his book of the same name. These gay éminences grises of music management make up an impressive list: Brian Epstein (the Beatles), Robert Stigwood (Cream and the Bee Gees), Simon Napier-Bell (the Yardbirds, Marc Bolan), Billy Gaff (Rod Stewart), and Ken Pitt (Bowie), to name but a few. Warhol performed this function for the Velvet Underground. Lesbians? Not so much, with the notable exception of Dusty Springfield, who was guided by the brilliant and well-respected Vicki Wickham.

These were intense and sometimes fraught relationships. The gay Svengalis—managers, agents, PR gurus—encouraged the flamboyant excesses of their long-haired foulard-wearing straight charges, while simultaneously living vicariously through them, and in some cases falling in love with them. Gay aesthetes like gallerist Robert Fraser and designer Christopher Gibbs, who basically invented the Swinging Sixties, were tight with the Beatles and the Stones, influencing everything from the look of their album covers to their home décor—Moroccan rugs! Hashish!—to their drugs of choice. Example: Fraser hooked the Beatles up with artists Peter Blake and Jann Haworth, who then created the cover for *Sgt. Pepper's*. Groovy Bob, as Fraser was known, was the first to champion Warhol in London.

The straight pop idols with their silky well-tended coiffures and their spanking new flowery shirts were met with official hostility from the stuffy establishment. But fans, especially female fans, and gays such as myself, bought their records and celebrated their tressy locks, Nehru jackets, and rebellious attitudes. Women throughout history have responded to androgyny in droves. The superstar castrati opera singers of the eighteenth century, such as Farinelli and Nicolini—the baroque version of

Bolan and Bowie—were mobbed from one end of Europe to the other. Fast-forward to glam rock. The nonthreatening sensitive bloke in the sequins, satin, and heavy makeup gives liberated girls permission to wear the pants, which they do. Two of the Spiders from Mars—Trevor Bolder and Mick Woodmansey—were initially reluctant to embrace the glam rock style, until they saw the effect it had on girls. This holds true today. When Harry Styles injects feminine allure into his stagecraft—I'm thinking of his gender-neutral palazzo pants, extra-long fluffy stage boas, and the ruffled frock he wore on the cover of *Vogue*—his feminine fan base cheers him on.

Back to 1972 and *Transformer*. Sparkling and sequined, Lou and Bowie go full nelly, expanding their fan base dramatically, while also causing great consternation among the older generation. Apparently these boys are not actually kidding. They mean it. Since they are both married, we are not entirely sure what "it" is, but it doesn't look much like conventional heterosexuality. The mysterious allure of androgyny resides in its ability to blur boundaries and create ambiguity. Arthur or Martha? Boris or Doris? Hmmm.

Between them, Bowie and Lou, in this historic year of dragtastic, glamtastic visibility, prod the sleeping giant and throw a feather boa round his/her/their neck. Their bitchy fem goalpost-moving bisexuality—or whatever the hell it is—penetrates the pop music arena and the global media. They are not saying, "See how much we act like poofs." They are saying, "We ARE poofs, or at least we might be, and if we are, there is nothing wrong with that. So there!" Female fans are fizzing, and queens such as myself are drenched with feelings of validation, recognition, and general euphoria. Their lack of clarity mirrors our own situation:

The whole notion of being out, coming out, had not taken hold. Most of us are still shadowboxing our way through life. But here's the good news: Being gay is no longer the tragic cul-de-sac that my dad outlined for me while pointing at Oscar Wilde's old hangout. Sexual deviation, as showcased in *Transformer*, is where it's at. But it's a big world out there. The wider reaction to this album is complex, to say the least.

Lou is now, as per his record company, RCA, the "Phantom of Rock," a musician with a face full of Max Factor and a fully orchestrated visual image. His association with Bowie—the pop-glam meteor who has harnessed the cultural moment and is working every angle—has brought Lou quick success. Dennis Katz and RCA send Lou off on a brutal tour, playing three to five concerts per week. Within a matter of months *Transformer* is a hit and Lou is mega.

Lou and Bettye get married. Bettye recalls her bridal outfit as follows: "I wore white satin bell-bottoms, a strand of classic pearls, a navy-blue cashmere sweater, and a smashing pair of red seriously high platform heels. Lou wore an all-white suit." It's noteworthy that he takes this very conventional step just at the time when he has become, in his fans' eyes, the patron saint of rule-breaking gender-fuck. Was Lou backing down? Bettye recalls Lou's new reality as follows: "The seats of Lou's shows were filling up with outsiders, the disenfranchised of society. As a result of 'Make Up' and 'Walk on the Wild Side,' gays, bisexuals, transvestites, and transsexuals flocked to Lou's shows, standing for hours in line for front row seats, dressed in the psychedelic outfits of the late '60s British Invasion."

According to Victor Bockris, Lou feels trapped: he fashioned himself in the image of what his English fans imagine he is, "a sexy wolverine, homosexual junkie hustler, and advocate of S & M."

Sounds good, right? But Lou is American. He has enjoyed a certain Dylan-esque gravitas in the US and is understandably anxious to maintain it. According to Bettye, it isn't the sexually transgressive stuff that irks him; it is the glam drag, which makes him "feel like a clown," which is a significant issue for a guy who has built his career on serious writing. Is the greatest songwriter of his age allowed to wear mascara? Fame and recognition have come for Lou Reed, but it doesn't feel so great. To quote Oscar Wilde: "When the gods wish to punish us they answer our prayers." For Lou and Bettye, there are some idyllic "perfect day" moments, but as Bettye notes in her memoir, "Fame is a fiend. It turns people into monsters."

In January of '73 Lou performs two major shows at Alice Tully Hall in Manhattan. According to Bettye, Lou is so anxious about this US *Transformer* launch that he embarks on a boozathon, and a cokathon, telling her, "I'm a failure and a fake and I don't deserve any of this." Playing in a band was one thing. Being a Ziggy, a tarted-up solo rock god is a whole other level of stress and scrutiny. As Peter Stanfield notes, "Lou outside of a band as a solo performer was at a loss."

These shows are sloppy, but sellouts. According to Anthony DeCurtis, a well-lubricated Lou tells a reporter, "That's why I don't give a fuck what the critics say. Fuck the critics." Andy attends the second show and shares his delight with Lou's success. He has a vested interest. Posters all over the subway promote Lou and, by association, Andy and his oeuvre. The publicity for Warhol's movies and his superstars generated indirectly by "Walk on the Wild Side" is significant.

Sales of *Transformer* peak six months after the November '72 launch, when the album goes platinum in the UK and reaches the #19 spot on the *Billboard* charts in the US, by which time

"Walk" has become the #1 jukebox hit in the USA. According to Lou, attempts to ban it are eventually stymied by fans, of all ages. Lou would recall in the taped Rotterdam conversation, "Little kids just loved to go doo-ta-doo. Little kids would call up stations and say, 'If you don't play it, I'll listen to another station.' So they had to unban it."

Does any of it make him happy? A couple of years later Lou admits to deriving genuine satisfaction from having expressed his solidarity with the LGBTQ+ community in such a bold fashion: "Do you know how many gay people were just so happy that somebody actually put this out?" he says to that friend in Rotterdam. This is unusual for him. Lou being Lou, it is hard for him to be sunny. When pals are sweet to him he turns on them. When the world throws bouquets at him he spits back. This is his nature. He reacts badly when people are nice. How about when they are vicious? Like, for example, the critics?

When it comes to *Transformer*, the reviewers are less than fawning. Their screeds are riddled with homophobic dog whistles, especially in the USA. How dare these modish glam rockers taint the world of classic rock with their posturing? Ellen Willis of *The New Yorker*, a longtime VU supporter, gives the album a scorching review: "What's the matter with Lou Reed? *Transformer* is terrible—lame, pseudo-decadent lyrics, lame, pseudo-something-or-other singing, and a just plain lame band." It's a shame that her three "lames" did not have a French accent on the last *e*. The message is clear: if you abandon your gritty heroin-infused downtown poetic roots for this fey bullshit, we will punish you. Willis later walked back some of her comments.

In *Rolling Stone*, Nick Tosches acknowledges the sexy sizzle of

"Hangin' 'Round," "Satellite of Love," "Vicious," and "Walk on the Wild Side," but adds, "Reed himself says he thinks the album's great. I don't think it's nearly as good as he's capable of doing. He seems to have the abilities to come up with some really dangerous, powerful music, stuff that people like Jagger and Bowie have only rubbed knees with."

In his Lou biography, Victor Bockris claims that Lisa and Richard Robinson, significant players in Lou's comeback and the making of the first solo album, are incensed with what they see as Lou's treacherous defection. They helped him get on his feet and hooked him up at RCA—they even introduced him to Bowie—and then, after that crummy first solo album, he left them in the dust. They lobby their contacts in the US to write negative reviews. According to Victor Bockris, Henry Edwards at the *New York Times* is persuaded to follow the Robinsons' edict. Edwards states, "I did what everybody else did—we fucked the album." Even the reviewers who give it a fair review gave the credit to Bowie and Ronno.

There are, it should be pointed out, some unqualified laudatory reviews: Ray Fox-Cumming, writing in *Disc*, describes *Transformer* as "a peep into a world that most of us would rather not experience firsthand, but it is presented with such humor and sympathy, without ever wallowing in the sadder aspects, that it's hugely enjoyable. A very stylish masterpiece."

Lou has been reading these publications for years, often enjoying their coverage of his work; now he sees many turn on him, simply because he disappeared to London for a few months and had a little fun and wore a little makeup and let Bowie and Ronno influence his creative process.

The negative response from writers who previously lauded his oeuvre must have been very painful for Lou. He is not a laugh-all-the-way-to-the-bank dude like Liberace or Gary Glitter. He is a serious poet with creative standing. The critical response to *Transformer* further enflames his existing antagonism toward journalists. On one occasion he instructs a scribe—Roy Hollingworth of *Melody Maker*—to refer to him as "a bisexual chauvinist pig," suggesting that he might be losing track of the nuanced messaging of this new fluid glam movement, or maybe he's simply making a blunt assessment of his own failings. One thing is clear: Lou is not feeling especially fabulous about Lou. He poignantly tells writer Michael Watts that he did not write a single song during his glam London sojourn.

The *Transformer* response confirms his commitment to poetic suffering. Lou is a fan of Charles Bukowski. In his booze-addled 1975 novel *Factotum* Bukowski delivers the following jeremiad: "If you're going to try, go all the way. Otherwise, don't even start. This could mean losing girlfriends, wives, relatives and maybe even your mind. It could mean not eating for three or four days. . . . It could mean jail. It could mean derision. It could mean mockery—isolation. Isolation is the gift. . . . You will ride life straight to perfect laughter. It's the only good fight there is." Maybe this whole jaunt to glam rock London was just too easy and too much fun? A cheap shot.

The retreat from glam was inevitable, especially for protean talents like Lou and Bowie, who were always pondering their next chapter. By the time Lou is raging on the *Billboard* charts, glam is also peaking. The music gods are already rummaging for the next big thing. Bowie has a little more carte blanche. He has made the genre his own and can stretch it out a bit with *Aladdin Sane*, recorded just before the release of *Transformer* and released the following April. On July 3, 1973, at a sold-out concert at the Hammersmith Odeon, Bowie dramatically announces his retirement. Is he Greta Garbo or what? I can remember the sinking feeling I experienced upon reading Charles Shaar Murray's account of the evening in *NME*. For a glam rock gay such as myself, it was right up there with the death of JFK. However—smiley face!—it turns out he just meant he was retiring Ziggy. Either way, the sound of screeching brakes is heard throughout the music industry. Glam rock? Maybe it wasn't the third generation of rock after all.

Around this time Bowie and Brian Ferry both release cover albums that are huge. Bowie's album *Pin Ups*, with its chic glam cover image shot by Justin de Villeneuve—Bowie and Twiggy wearing mask makeup by Pierre Laroche, who also created the *Aladdin Sane* lightning bolt on Bowie's face—is dripping with camp and '60s nostalgia. *Pin Ups* is not only a nifty work of creative pastiche but also a great way for Bowie to hit the pause button while he figures out his next incarnation. Unsurprisingly, the reviews for *Pin Ups* are ghastly. The rock press consistently bashes anything deemed accessible, playful, or fashiony. But the general public could not care less. *Pin Ups* is still one of Bowie's top sellers. This period of glam hate is a warm-up for the "Disco sucks!" movement, the racist and homophobic backlash that will see hard rock fans attempting to expunge anything less than butch from the airwaves. (More on this later.)

Imagine if Lou had put together a cover album like *Pin Ups*? A Jacques Brel song? A Bacharach here, a Beatles there, possibly with Cale and a VU member or two? Lou and Iggy doing an Everly Brothers favorite? But Lou, poet that he is, has renewed his focus on gravitas. No more creative shortcuts to stardom.

Ere long, Lou backs away from Bowie: "I'm not going in the same direction as David. . . . I wanted to try that heavy eye makeup and dance about a bit . . . Anyway, I've done it all now and stopped it." His next album, *Berlin*, is released eleven months after *Transformer*. It's a total volte-face. With *Berlin* Lou takes the unfolding misery of his relationship with Bettye and creates a concept album. The themes are prostitution, spousal abuse, depression, and suicide. (And you thought your great-uncle Irving was dour.) This album is an exquisite Rorschach test. My depressive female straight pals love it and still play it on rainy afternoons. My frothy gays? Not so much. Lou describes it to journalist Lester Bangs as "a backlash on *Transformer*. Maybe I'll do a song on it called 'Get Back in the Closet, You Fuckin' Queers.'"

Lest you take umbrage, let me reassure that Lou is just being a hyperbolic thirty-year-old contrarian rock star. He has no intention of shoving the gays back in their fancy armoires. He quickly qualifies the cheeky statement as follows: "I just think that everyone's into this scene because it's supposedly the thing to do right now. . . . You just can't fake being 'gay.' If they claim they're gay, they're going to have to make love in a gay style. And most of them aren't capable of making that commitment." What is Lou really saying about his own proclivities? He appears to be making a distinction between styling oneself gay and the real nitty-gritty. *There are people who pretend to be gay, but, when push comes to shove, they can neither push nor shove, and, by the way, I, Lou Reed, happen not to be one of them.*

In summation, the critics' reaction to *Transformer* is brutal. The civilian reaction is explosive and positive—the biggest hits of his career—and brings a new level of fame to Lou while simultaneously forcing him to question his creative integrity and reconsider his artistic identity. The LGBTQ+ reaction is delirious and forever. For us gays it's like a massive dose of Zoloft, decades before it's invention.

And, most important of all, what about Lou's drag queens? How did they cope with their global jukebox superstardom? From one end of the USA to the other Candy is now known as a blow-job-dispensing backroom floozy. Is she still digging it? Lou has sung about her before, inserting a poignant line in the song "Candy Says," on the third VU album: "I've come to hate my body / And all that it requires in this world." Lou would later recall Candy's desire to take the Lou Reed show on the road as follows: "Candy Darling told me he'd [sic] memorized all the songs and wanted to make a *Candy Darling Sings Lou Reed* album."

Jackie Curtis became James Dean, for more than a day. According to Craig Highberger's biography of her, *Superstar in a Housedress*, it was an entire year. She later clarified that she had become tired of being Jackie Curtis: ". . . it was a chore. And I was already turning my auto-suggestive possession into a reincarnation of James Dean, so I became him." And the speed addiction that had now been disclosed to millions of people? Jackie had bigger wigs to fry. She recalled, "Within just a couple of years my mother died, my grandmother died, my Uncle Tony died, and I had to send Uncle Jackie to a state institution. It was just too much for me, so there was nothing else to do but put on the dress and the glamour and the mink and go the curb and scream 'Taxi!' and go to work."

And Holly? Did she come to regret her leg-shaving inclusion in "Walk"? "My parents heard it in Florida! The fact that it's a classic, it makes my panties twitter."

The only person whose panties are not twittering is Lou. As

Bettye succinctly observes in her memoir *Perfect Day*, "He felt he was betraying himself, and he began to resent playing some of these songs, which he also considered somewhat frivolous." Like I said, Lou was cursed with a heavy brain.

As a postscript to this chapter I need to acknowledge that not every member of the LGBTQ+ community was banging a tambourine and hanging out the bunting. Some had heavy brains just like Lou. Many civilian reactions to *Transformer* were more nuanced and complex than my own. How could they have been otherwise when it teased such taboo subject matter? While many gay people greeted Lou's gay album as an engraved invitation to a Mardi Gras, others in the LGBTQ+ monde endured a more uncomfortable response.

In 2022 *Vanity Fair* described trans woman Lucy Sante as "a renowned writer, culture critic, and scholar of the demimonde." In 1972 Lucy, by her own telling, was still Luc, a bewildered brilliant lad, hiding his roiling trans impulses from his religious mother and playing hooky from his Jesuit high school on the Upper East Side of Manhattan. On paper Luc was the target audience for *Transformer*, an inveterate Velvet Underground fan who was (quoting Lucy from my own conversation with her today) "mesmerized by the Gesamtkunstwerk of the band" and thought Lou was "talented as fuck. I loved the dark glasses and leather. The perfect urban armor, like a French New Wave movie. I felt I was in direct dialogue with him. I was even rewriting the lyrics to 'Sister Ray.'" The arrival of *Transformer* should have been, if there was any justice in the world, his engraved invitation.

In 2022, having finally made her transition, Lucy now recalls the experience as follows: "Back then I treated *Transformer* like kryptonite. I avoided it because it represented this thing that I was trying to suppress. In 1972 I was eighteen. It was an extremely vulnerable period. I'd had two horrific acid trips, both gender themed. This was the most fraught period of my life because of the unresolved trans stuff." The success of "Walk on the Wild Side," purring and taunting out of every car radio and jukebox, added to the agony: "This song went through me like a knife, on a regular basis. Now, fifty years later, it's on my shelf, deracinated, staring at me. And I stare back."

Candy Darling in 1971. "I'm a thousand different people. Every one is real."

(Kenn Duncan, New York Public Library archive)

CHAPTER 8

Aftermath

AUSTRALIAN JOURNALIST: Are you a transvestite or a homosexual?
LOU REED: Sometimes.

It's been half a century since the debut of *Transformer*. How did things play out in those five ensuing decades? Did that moment of gay audacity and visibility fulfill its promise? The answer is simple: yes, no, and, just like Lou, sometimes.

Yes, we now inhabit a more groovy, accepting world, but it was by no means a straight shot. The journey toward enlightenment and acceptance—there is no question that *Transformer* played a role in this process—has encountered many blips and belches and potholes since 1972.

The decade descends rapidly into financial stagnation, paranoia, Watergate, urban decay, and domestic terrorist bombings instigated by various groups, including the Weathermen in the US and the IRA in the UK, but other than that, everything is just fanfucking-tastic.

On February 4, 1974, Patty Hearst, the granddaughter of newspaper publisher William Randolph Hearst, is kidnapped from her apartment in Berkeley, California, by a radical group calling themselves the Symbionese Liberation Army. Fun fact: Richard Berlin, the father of Brigid—the Warhol insider who taped Lou's last concert with the Velvets—held the purse strings at the mighty Hearst corporation and oversaw the ransom demands of the SLA.

One month later Candy Darling dies of lymphoma, aged twenty-nine. Before shuffling off her mortal coil, Candy poses exquisitely on her deathbed for photographer Peter Hujar. The resulting glamour shots show Candy as she would like us to remember her, fully coiffed and made-up, surrounded by ramparts of roses, ready for her close-up, every inch the movie star.

On September 13, 1974, LaBelle launch their album *Nightbirds*, introducing us to "Lady Marmalade" and the sex-positive gentility of the phrase "*Voulez-vous coucher avec moi ce soir?*" In their extraordinary quilted sculptural Larry LeGaspi space-glam costumes and headdresses and their metallic maquillage, Patti Labelle, Nona Hendryx, and Sarah Dash approach their onstage presentation with the same outrageous bravado as any of the male glam rockers. They also bridge the gap between glam rock and funk. In the intervening years Nona Hendryx has become a gay rights activist. Hey, sista, soul sista. LaBelle was managed by the fabulous Vicki Wickham, Dusty Springfield's former manager, and Nona Hendryx's life partner.

Lou's war with journalists heats up. In 1975 the late great Lester Bangs pens an immediately infamous gonzo-style interview with Lou for *Creem* magazine titled "Let Us Now Praise Famous Death Dwarves; or, How I Slugged It Out with Lou Reed and Stayed Awake." Lester claims that Lou is his hero because he "stands for all the most fucked-up things that I could ever conceive of. Which probably only shows the limit of my imagination." Lou holds his own in the brawl with Lester, as exemplified by the following: "You really are an asshole. You went past assholism into some kinda urinary tract."

Combative rock journalism may be soaring, but the art market is financially depressed. At Warhol's Factory, things keep chugging along. Andy creates an important series of trans artworks. I refer to

Ladies and Gentlemen, 1975, the brilliantly titled series of silkscreens of Black trans women. Marsha P. Johnson, of Stonewall fame, is in the mix.

Speaking of trans women: In 1975 Lou gets a new girlfriend named Rachel Humphreys. Rachel, a hairdresser from Philly, arrived in New York in 1970. Looking to elevate herself, she began to frequent Max's Kansas City, and eventually found Lou. Danny Fields recalls this relationship as follows: "She was so beautiful and vulnerable. They loved each other. Tragic lovers."

Jeremy Reed's biography of Lou titled *Waiting for the Man* describes this amour fou in some detail. Since Lou wholeheartedly endorsed Jeremy's work—"All the books about me are bullshit except Jeremy's"—his account is worth a look. Jeremy Reed describes Rachel as "a stunning Mexican-Indian transvestite who identified as female" but was "resistant to gender reassignment surgery." J. R. sees their relationship as "a de facto gay partnership that had survived five years of chronic speed and alcohol on Reed's distempered, resolutely self-destructive part." They live in Lou's Upper East Side apartment, festooned with red velvet, Lou's gold records, a pair of antelope horns, and a zebra rug slung across the floor. Lou wears Rachel's fashion tops, ceases dying his hair blond, and becomes, as per Jeremy Reed, "a Biba black Rachel clone."*

The union proves symbiotic, providing Rachel with a better life and Lou with an emotional security that fuels his creativity. When Mick Rock interviews Lou for *Penthouse*, Lou talks about life with Rachel in glowing terms: "There's someone hustling around for

---

* Biba: the art-deco-inspired London fashion store known for black-clad smoky-eyed vampy salesgirls and clients.

me I can totally trust." After encountering Warhol's pet dachshund, the couple acquire a pair of their own, naming them the Baron and the Duke. They are often seen promenading with their boys in Washington Square.

Lou memorializes the relationship with the album *Coney Island Baby*, a love poem to Rachel, recorded in 1975. Jeremy Reed describes the title song as "a celebratory and surprising nostalgic tribute to Rachel, saturated in the intensity of Lou's feelings for his new partner and the realization that the redemptive 'glory of love' is a transcendent thing that gets above suffering." This album, Rachel's homage, puts Lou back in the *Billboard* top 20. Despite being his muse, Rachel is not a fan of Lou's music. Lou seems amused by this fact, telling Jeremy Reed, "Rachel loves disco music and Diana Ross." At this time, in that 1975 Netherlands taped conversation with his friend, Lou states, "I always meet the people I'm supposed to." It's a safe bet that he would include Rachel in that assessment.

Also in 1975: Lou puts out a challenging, how-not-to-have-a-hit record titled *Metal Machine Music*, a double album of abstract guitar distortion. Not exactly easy-listening. Lou is clearly retaining the right to "leave people wanting less." In the liner notes Lou claims that *Metal Machine Music* is the ultimate and final expression of heavy metal music. Insane, yes, but in the aftermath of *Transformer*, there is a logic to it. Lou is underscoring his avant-garde bona fides, and reminding the audience that he and the Velvets were the first to marry pop music with experimental music.

In 1977 punk explodes in the UK. Punk rockers love the Velvet Underground, most especially Lou. As a result I have, for decades, been laboring under the delusion that Sid Vicious (né John Ritchie) named himself after Lou's *Transformer* song. The truth is more picaresque. Apparently Johnny Rotten nicknamed Ritchie "Sid

Vicious" after Rotten's pet hamster Sid, named after Pink Floyd's Syd Barrett, had sunk his teeth into Ritchie. "Sid is really vicious!" opined Ritchie, and the rest is hamster history.

Meanwhile uptown, Studio 54 opens its doors. Warhol becomes a relentless habitué and begins to mirror the brittle name-dropping glamour of this world—Liza! Halston! Bianca! Mick! Jerry!—in his silkscreened artworks and in the pages of *Interview* magazine.

In 1978 Sugar Plum Fairy's ex-boyfriend, gay rights pioneer and former San Francisco Board of Supervisors member Harvey Milk, along with SF mayor George Moscone are assassinated, just one year after Milk became California's first openly gay elected official. The gunman is disgruntled former supervisor Dan White, whose lawyer manages to get his sentence reduced to voluntary manslaughter. I am living in LA at the time—at the sleazy Tropicana Motel where the VU stayed in the mid-'60s—in an apolitical bubble, but even I feel convulsed by the injustice of this. Yes, Dan White also murdered straight Moscone, but it's hard to shake the notion that this is a case of it's-okay-to-shoot-a-fag. This is a huge blow to gay civil rights. There is a feeling that Anita Bryant and other anti-gay crusaders are successfully turning back the clock.

More bad news: "Disco sucks!" takes off. A Detroit rock radio DJ named Steve Dahl is so angered by the fact that Led Zeppelin and various other rock bands are being elbowed out to make room for increasingly popular artists like Donna Summer, the Village People, and Chic, he unleashes a "Disco sucks!" movement. Dahl invites like-minded spirits to phone in their disco requests, which he then obliterates on air with ear-splitting explosions. In July 1979 Dahl lets it be known that anyone in possession of a disco record will receive discounted entry to the White Sox home game in Chicago's Comiskey Park. Almost sixty thousand show up, burn records, and seriously lose their sangfroid. It's a riot. The dog-whistle subtext is transparent: disco is the music of homosexuals and Black people.

That same year journalist Stephen Demorest asks Lou how he feels about having grown up closeted. He replies, "I resent it. It was a very big drag. From age thirteen I could have been having a ball and not even thought about this shit. What a waste of time. If the forbidden thing is love, you spend most of your time playing with hate. Who needs that? I feel I was gypped."

The decade ends with a bang, in the face, for Bowie. Lou and Bowie are hanging out in a London restaurant after a Bowie concert. An inebriated Lou asks Bowie if he would be interested in producing his ninth album. Bowie says yes, on condition that Lou cleans up his act and gets sober. (Bowie has recently kicked his cocaine habit and has sobriety on his mind.) This sends Reed into a rage and he starts boxing Bowie in the face and has to be pulled off. Insults are traded and continue back at the hotel, in the corridor. I'm sorry I missed it.

In 1980, on Valentine's Day, Lou marries wife number two, a beautiful girl named Sylvia Morales. She becomes his longtime companion, sobriety support, graphics genius, and manager. They divorce in 1994. She subsequently is very protective of his legacy, telling the *New York Times* in 2015 that he was never physically aggressive with her. "He saw things differently," she says. "He was a creative genius." Ms. Morales characterizes her Lou experience as follows: "In the years that I lived and worked with him, he had no diagnosis of severe mental illness, no hospitalizations, no admissions to clinics, no depressive states, no interventions, no withdrawals into apathy. He was constantly productive and working."

Also in the *New York Times*: On July 3, 1981, an article carries the headline "Rare Cancer Seen in 41 Homosexuals." The CDC reports clusters of Kaposi's sarcoma and *Pneumocystis carinii* pneumonia among gay men in California and New York City. AIDS will darken the skies over the '80s, killing six hundred thousand Americans, including many of my close friends and ex-boyfriends. The gruesome nature of AIDS—the agony, the disfigurement, the biblical sense of shame—dictates that there is no longer any cachet in, as Bowie and Reed did, expressing bisexuality or gay solidarity, or teasing the press with suggestions that you might be gay. With a gay plague looming, nobody is lining up to queer identify. What was cool and fresh in the early '70s becomes a tale of Typhoid Marys. Boy George and Marc Almond, amongst others, are both warned by their record companies to NEVER mention the G word, especially if they hope to find success in the US. AIDS provides cheap ammunition to anti-gay campaigners, allowing them to consolidate their positions.

Despite the backdrop of AIDS—a holocaust for gay men of my generation—the 1980s proves to be a fecund innovative decade, producing a gorgeous collision of rap, graffiti, art, fashion, music, scratching, breaking. At the end of the previous decade, punk administered a giant enema to the culture, and now anything, musically and creatively, is possible. The early '80s give us Devo, Joy Division, Kraftwerk, Depeche Mode, the Human League, the Psychedelic Furs, Nina Hagen, and so many rule-breaking lunatics. Though they are low-key about their sexual preferences, a world of LGBTQ+ creatives find their voice producing a fabulous outpouring of androgynous magic. I'm talking about Culture Club and Boy George, Soft Cell, Marilyn, Pete Burns of Dead or Alive, Annie Lennox, and Grace Jones. And let's not forget the whole New Romantic movement, also known as the Cult with No Name—as exemplified by Spandau Ballet, Steve Strange and Visage, Adam Ant, and myself. I am a full participant in this costumed madness—I spend many months dressed as a pirate—resulting in being cast in the video for Kim Carnes's "Bette Davis Eyes." (I'm wearing the wiggly patterned Vivienne Westwood pirate shirt.) Bowie and Lou are the grandfathers of this movement. Lou steers clear, but Bowie releases "Ashes to Ashes," dons a clown costume, and joins the masquerade.

In June 1984 Bronski Beat—all gay and out—have a synth-pop chart hit with "Smalltown Boy." Lou releases six albums in the '80s. Though he stays true to his roots as a poetic outsider with such records as *The Blue Mask* and *New York,* he has yet to figure out how to raise his profile by using MTV. He needs a Warhol or a Bowie to propel him into the visual realm. One suspects, however, that he is happier being Lou, a middle-aged poet of forty-two, pursuing his own authentic path.

Also in 1984, Queen have a hit with "I Want to Break Free." The lads have a blast filming the accompanying video, which is intended to be a good-natured parody of UK soap *Coronation Street.* They wear tarty working-class drag, head to foot. Everyone gets the joke, except in Brazil, where rocks are thrown, and North America, where, as Brian May recalls, "people turned ashen," causing MTV to ban the video, thereby making a significant dent in Queen's US commercial viability.

Freddie was never really able to come out during his lifetime. He confined any expressions of gayness to his performances. Since Queen was a bona fide rock band, it was too risky to ally himself with gay causes. He left the planet in 1991, the first major rock star to die of AIDS.

More deaths: Jackie Curtis expires from a heroin overdose in 1985. Obits reveal the astonishing fact that Jackie was married six times, so maybe we should not overinterpret the significance of marriages such as Lou's and Bowie's, back in the '70s and '80s. My personal favorite Jackie memory comes from *Women in Revolt.* After giving a tiresome, laborious blow job to Mr. America, Jackie delivers an unforgettable brilliant ad lib that is pure Jackie: "This can't be what millions of girls commit suicide over after their boyfriends leave them . . ."

Warhol dies from gallbladder complications on February 22, 1987, at age fifty-eight. Andy once said, "I don't believe in death, because I always think that when somebody dies they actually just go uptown . . . They go to Bloomingdale's and they just take a little longer to get back." Whenever I go to Bloomingdale's I always wonder if I am going to run into Andy.

Warhol's death brings together Lou Reed and John Cale. At the Saint Patrick's Cathedral memorial they chat for the first time in years. The renewed connection leads to a collaboration album, *Songs for Drella*, a melancholy tribute to their fallen Svengali. Andy's Factory nickname was Drella—a contraction of Dracula (blood sucking) and Cinderella (sweetness personified). Warhol disliked the name, which is probably why it stuck. The two sides of the Warhol coin facilitated his success. Might Lou have been a happier dude if he had had a Cinderella side, as opposed to his Hydra of different personalities? But then he wouldn't have been Lou.

In the summer of 1988, Nico, on vacation in Ibiza, sets off to buy pot, falls off her bicycle, and dies from a brain injury.

In 1989 Lou releases *New York*, an album that includes a lament titled "Halloween Parade," a beautiful dirge for those who have died of AIDS. Lou struggled to do happy. He never had a problem doing sad. Selecting the Halloween parade as a living metaphor was a brilliant choice. Every gay man of my generation has a bundle of snaps of men, costumed for Halloween, who did not live long enough to become blasé about the Halloween parade.

The following year, Rachel Humphreys, Lou's beautiful, mysterious Coney Island baby, is felled by AIDS, aged thirty-seven.

In 1990 "Walk on the Wild Side" is gorgeously sampled on a hip-hop song called "Can I Kick It?" by legends A Tribe Called Quest. Over the last fifty years "Walk" has been covered and performed by a massive number of diverse talents including, but not limited to, Herbie Mann, Vanessa Paradis, Suzanne Vega, Romy Haag, Edie Brickell, and Justin Vivian Bond (Kiki of Kiki and Herb.)

Lou hits his stride with the 1992 release of *Magic and Loss*, his best-reviewed album since *Transformer*. Dear reader, I highly recommend that you take a moment to watch the official video for the song "What's Good" whilst reading the lyrics. Lou features an impressively leonine mullet. In addition to enjoying his hairstyle, you will be reminded of his idiosyncratic writerly genius and why he was so influential to everyone from Morrissey to REM to the Arctic Monkeys. Bono once said from the stage, "Every song we've ever written was a rip-off of a Lou Reed song." This album is a reminder of his talent, which was not contingent on Cale or Bowie. To quote the tweet of Julian Casablancas of the Strokes, "Lou is the reason I do everything that I do," or as he elaborated "he's on the Mount Rushmore of rad dudes."

In 1992 Marsha P. Johnson's body is found floating in the East River. The mystery of her death has yet to be solved. One year later Mick Ronson dies of liver cancer, aged forty-six.

In 1996 Lou, John Cale, and Maureen Tucker play together one more time while being inducted into the Rock and Roll Hall of Fame. Danny Fields describes Maureen Tucker as "down to Earth, realistic, the record-keeper of the band, with a large Southern family, the matriarch."

In 1997 *Transformer* is named the 44th greatest album of all time in a UK "Greatest of the Millennium" poll. That same year Lou and Bowie make up enough for Reed to play Bowie's fiftieth birthday. Bowie pours forth arrangements of Reed's songs that are pure Las Vegas camp. Their entente cordiale may well be connected to Lou's nouveau sobriety. He is now finding solace in tai chi, a practice that will continue to his deathbed.

Meanwhile, at the 1998 Eurovision song contest, an augur of the new era of trans acceptance that will come to dominate the early twenty-first century: Dana International from Israel is the first trans woman to enter *and win* the Eurovision song contest.

The new century brings a renewed appreciation for *Transformer*. In 2000 it is voted #58 in *Encyclopedia of Popular Music* founder Colin Larkin's *All-Time Top 1000 Albums*. *New Musical Express* in the UK ranks it #55 on their Greatest Albums of All Time list. *Rolling Stone* ranks it #194 of 500 Greatest Albums of All Time. The year 2002 sees the release of a thirtieth anniversary edition of *Transformer*.

Doubts about Lou's iconic status will be vanquished when you watch Lou and Pavarotti sing a duet of "Perfect Day." The highest Himalayan camp. So ridiculous, but by the end of it you are reaching for the Kleenex. Like I already told you, camp is "the lie that tells the truth."

In 2004 *Rolling Stone* publishes a retrospective review of *Transformer* that is loaded with grudging praise for Lou, who "wrote a bunch of clever new songs and tried to cash in on producer David Bowie's trendily androgynous glam rock, which worked well enough to break 'Walk on the Wild Side.'"

They say that flecks of glitter never biodegrade and will therefore never leave the planet. Ditto glam rock, the gift that keeps on giving. In 2007, glamdrogynous Verka Serduchka—representing Ukraine and dressed as a human disco ball—blows up at the Eurovision song contest and becomes an LGBTQ+ icon.

On April 24, 2008, Lou Reed marries his long-term partner, experimental music legend Laurie Anderson, in a private ceremony in Colorado. Previously, in 2003, the couple had appeared together, with their little doggie, on Charlie Rose's chat show. It is evident from their sweetness and their touches—Lou caresses Laurie, while Laurie caresses the dog—that he has found another sympatico soul mate. This vignette is a reminder that Lou was never a loner. He was always happiest in a pack, even a small pack of three. Andy once said, "People have so many problems with love, always looking for someone to be their Via Veneto, their soufflé that can't fail." One hopes they were each other's unfailing soufflé.

In 2009 Obama lifts the twenty-two-year ban on admitting people to the US with HIV. From my perspective this represents massive progress. I came to the US in the 1970s, when gay people, pre-AIDS, were formally excluded from immigrating. No fageles allowed. I vividly remember doing my best imitation of an aggressive straight boy when the immigration official began to insist that I was gay and therefore disqualified from receiving a green card: "Yeah! I like birds, don't I?" So, yes, there has been enormous progress. I have vada'd it with my own ogles. (Translation from Polari: I have seen it with my own eyes.)

Lou Reed's final years are full of creativity and collaboration, including theatre productions with Robert Wilson and—gasp—an album with Metallica. The Metallica collaboration comes about after Lou and the boys perform "Sweet Jane" together at the twenty-fifth-anniversary Hall of Fame show. *This* is a truly great rock and roll moment. Total chills. On October 31, 2011, Lou and Metallica release *Lulu*. When I first heard the title I got completely the wrong impression. Remembering that Lulu was Lou's nickname in the Factory days, I assumed he was somehow exploring those swishy halcyon times with Drella and Holly and Candy and Jackie. No such luck. *Lulu*, a truly esoteric enterprise, consists of Lou reading from an obscure French poem while the boys heroically pound their instruments. One wag suggested it sounded like Homer Simpson yelling over a soundtrack of construction work. David Brendel, who worked with Laurie Anderson and Lou's musical right-hand Hal Willner on the creation of a book that accompanied a boxed set of Lou's solo work, recalls the advent of *Lulu* as follows: "The collaboration was seen as a terrible idea by both Lou fans and Metallica fans—who were often in separate camps. Collaborating with a heavy-metal band was not perceived as avant-garde; if anything it was misinterpreted as a commercial ploy, and a bad one at that. The record began to get vicious reviews online before they'd even begun to record it. Post-release, Lou loved to watch YouTube clips of bitter Metallica fans ranting about how much they despised *Lulu*. He'd watch his favorite attacks again and again, reveling with glee."

October 27, 2013, Lou Reed dies, aged seventy-one. At Lou's 2015 posthumous Hall of Fame induction ceremony, Laurie Anderson, in her acceptance speech, says the following: "After Lou's death David Bowie made a big point of saying to me, 'Listen. *Lulu* is Lou's greatest work. It is his masterpiece.'"

Bowie, who also became more experimental as he approached death, is paying Lou a serious posthumous compliment. He is giving it up to Lou for sticking to his avant-garde vision. Post-*Transformer*, Lou's output remained doggedly that of a poet and an uncompromising artist. The fact that some of those albums might leave you, as per Warhol's edict, wanting less is irrelevant. The point is that Lou never stopped walking on the wild side of his creative imagination.

Opinions vary about *Transformer*. One thing is undeniable: as intended, the album touched the LGBTQ+ monde and continues to do so. Another thing is certain: this album was the catalyst that helped Lou figure out who he was, and what felt wrong, and what felt right, and why mascara and sequins were not his jam, and why it was so important for him to cling to his inner Delmore Schwartz and his Bukowski, and to not chase flash or commercialism, and to dig his (unvarnished) fingernails into his outsider poetic vision and cling on tight. Yes, *Transformer* brought him the cash that allowed him to focus on his poetry and his cred, but one suspects he would have done it anyway, in a garret on the Lower East Side, tossing old chair legs into a wood-burning stove and throwing his poo out the window. (Metaphorically, of course.)

I never met Lou, but we did have a close encounter.

In 2010, Lou is seated at the next lunch table at Café Cluny in Greenwich Village. I am trying to keep my composure, but it's not easy. Lou occupies a mythological place in my psyche and that of many millions. Over the decades he has maintained his enigma. Lou represents so many archetypes. He is the lady in the tower. The tortured artist. He is the lost boy. The rock and roll animal, the phantom, the Frankenstein, the Adonis. And now, in late middle age, he has become the sacred cow. And let's not forget that Hydra with all those different personalities.

Today he is the Medusa, a castrating kvetch, having a classic Lou Reed meltdown. He is directing his ire at his squirming lunch companions. It's impossible to tell what has triggered this loss of equanimity. One thing is for certain. Lou is pissed.

This is not such a big surprise to me. His reputation for cantankerous behavior is part of his legend. I met Iggy and Bowie and found them both easy-breezy cover girl, and great conversationalists. Lou has always seemed taciturn, and proud of it. His general vibe is a clear disinvitation to bullshit and kissy-kissy. I am also aware that, on the plus side, Lou has been extraordinarily philanthropic in recent years, supporting friends and strangers alike.

As I observe his Cluny freak-out I find it heartening to know that he still has it in him to lose his shit. I want to shout, "You go, girl!"

I am far more concerned about the way my (younger) dining companions react. They seem genuinely alarmed to discover Lou's grumpy side and are prepared to write him off on this basis. It is apparent to me that they want him to be something or somebody that he is not. Their understanding of what makes a great artist seems, dare I say it, a tad limited.

They, with commendable idealism, would prefer him to be an avuncular rock 'n' roll benefactor, a role model, all sweetness and light, an arm-around-the-shoulder parental figure who will sign an autograph and maybe help them score an internship. The inability to accept him warts and all saddens me.

We now live in an era when being nice has become more important than being yourself. Great artists are now consigned to the trash heap based on their past transgressions, great and small. Being a hell-raiser, a Ginger Baker, or an Axl Rose or a Janice or an Ari Up—a flawed unapologetic creative tour de force, incapable of winning Miss Congeniality contests—has gone out of fashion. This is a shame. As Flaubert said, "You don't make art out of good intentions."

So, dear reader, if you find yourself struggling to reconcile the different facets of an artist such as Lou, take a deep breath and remember that you are not alone. These uncomfortable gnashings and gnawings are an unavoidable consequence of fandom. My advice to those wrestling with the tricky evil-or-genius contradictions in Lou's story is to compartmentalize the ghastly aspects of his story—I am thinking in particular about his treatment of Bettye—but not, under any circumstances, to deny their existence. As Danny Fields so succinctly stated in a postmortem assessment of Lou's contradictions in the *New York Times*, titled "Who Was the

Real Lou Reed?," "Most talented people are horrible and wonderful simultaneously."

Great art often comes from nightmares, warts, conflicts, and brutality. Lou's life was lived in service to his art, and we are the beneficiaries. And, most important, he was good to the outliers and the LGBTQ+ community. Isn't that enough, fer chrissakes? Or does he still need to be Mr. Rogers as well? David Brendel shares my fervor on this issue: "Lou's irreverence was the main thing which lured me as a teenager. His hostility helped me feel defiant about being an outsider."

Critics still take the occasional whizz on *Transformer*, but the record-buying public dig it, and will always take pleasure from hearing those *do-de-do*s and the glam-rocking songs that made the world a less dreary place for so many. At the time of writing, four tracks on *Transformer* have accumulated over half a billion plays on Spotify. Add all the other streaming services plus CD and vinyl and you have all the evidence you need. As Lou so succinctly put it, "Fuck the critics." This album is now the sole property of us fans, us civilians, us walkers on the wild side. And, like Proud Mary, it just keeps on rolling.

Paying homage to *Transformer* on a BBC documentary titled *Lou Reed Remembered*, Boy George declared the following: "If you're a quirky kid, in ten years' time you will find *Transformer*. It might be in your dad's record collection, or your grandfather's record collection, whatever, but if you've got an ear for music, it will resonate with you, and that's the power of great music."

RIP, Lulu. And thank you.

Acknowledgments

Massive gratitude to all the Lou lovers who allowed me to pick their lovely brains for this book: Danny Fields—legend!—fashion/culture commentator Paul Gorman, fashion writer Tim Blanks, photographer Karl Stoecker, Betsey Johnson and her biographer Mark Vitulano, Lucy Sante and Peter Stanfield, author of the magnificent tome *Pin-Ups 1972*. Thanks to Jeremy Reed, whose painstaking account of Lou's relationship with trans woman Rachel Humphreys in his fab book *Waiting for the Man* fills a significant gap in LGBTQ+ history.

Photographers: Thanks to Nat Finkelstein, Michael Putland, Diana Davies, Jack Mitchell, Kenn Duncan, and the incredible Mick Rock, RIP. A massive shout-out to Dustin Pittman for his magnificent cover image and for sharing his personal recollections of Lou.

Thanks to my editor, Elizabeth Mitchell, at HarperOne for hatching this idea and inviting me to write this book, and to Ghjulia Romiti for all her assistance. Thanks to Mari Moriarty, Deb Hayes, husbear Jonathan Adler, and David Brendel for all the invaluable feedback. Huge bravos to copy editor Dianna Stirpe (sorry about the mangled tenses) and book designer Leah Carlson-Stanisic.

Thanks to Laurie Anderson and the Lou Reed estate for donating his papers to the New York Public Library, thereby sending Lou back to the people.

Bibliography

. . . in no particular order with the exception of the first four books—Holly, Jackie, Candy, and Andy—which are not only amusing, but foundational to the tale of *Transformer*.

Holly Woodlawn with Jeffrey Copeland, *A Low Life in High Heels: The Holly Woodlawn Story* (New York: St Martin's, 1991)

Craig B. Highberger, *Superstar in a House Dress: The Life and Legend of Jackie Curtis* (New York: Chamberlain Brothers, 2005)

Candy Darling, *My Face for the World to See: The Diaries, Letters, and Drawings of Candy Darling, Andy Warhol Superstar* (Honolulu: Hardy Marks, 1997)

Andy Warhol, *The Philosophy of Andy Warhol (From A to B and Back Again)* (New York: Harcourt Brace Jovanovich, 1975)

Victor Bockris, *Transformer: The Complete Lou Reed Story* (London: HarperCollins, 2014)

Barney Hoskyns, *Glam! Bowie, Bolan, and the Glitter Rock Revolution* (London: Faber and Faber, 1998)

Ken Scott and Robert Owsinski, *Abbey Road to Ziggy Stardust: Off the Record with the Beatles, Bowie, Elton, and So Much More* (Los Angeles: Alfred Music, 2012)

Bettye Kronstad, *Perfect Day: An Intimate Portrait of Life with Lou Reed* (London: Jawbone, 2016)

Lester Bangs, *Psychotic Reactions and Carburetor Dung*, edited by Greil Marcus (New York: A. A. Knopf, 1987)

Peter Stanfield, *Pin-Ups 1972: Third Generation Rock 'n' Roll* (London: Reaktion Books, 2022)

Sasha Geffen, *Glitter Up the Dark: How Pop Music Broke the Binary* (Austin: Univ. of Texas Press, 2020)

Nick Kent, *The Dark Stuff: Selected Writings on Rock Music 1972–1993* (London: Faber and Faber, 2007)

Angela Bowie with Patrick Carr, *Backstage Passes: Life on the Wild Side with David Bowie* (London: Orion, 1993)

Darryl W. Bullock, *The Velvet Mafia: The Gay Men Who Ran the Swinging Sixties* (London: Omnibus, 2021)

Charles Shaar Murray, *Shots from the Hip: Notes from the Counterculture* (Ipswitch, UK: Aaaargh! Press, 1991)

Anthony DeCurtis, *Lou Reed: A Life* (New York: Little, Brown, 2017)

Ezra Furman, *Transformer* (New York: Bloomsbury Academic, 2018)

Paul Gorman, *Mr. Freedom: Tommy Roberts: British Design Hero* (Croydon, UK: Adelita, 2012)

Paul Gorman, *The Look: Adventures in Rock and Pop Fashion* (Croydon, UK: Adelita, 2006)

Philip Core, *Camp: The Lie That Tells the Truth* (London: Plexus, 1984)

Steven Watson, *Factory Made: Warhol and the Sixties* (New York: Pantheon, 2003)

Victor Bockris and Gerard Malanga, *Uptight: The Velvet Underground Story* (London: Omnibus Press, 2009)

Roger Griffin, *David Bowie: The Golden Years* (London: Omnibus Press, 2016)

Legs McNeill, *Please Kill Me: The Uncensored Oral History of Punk* (New York: Grove Press, 2016)

Jeremy Reed, *Waiting for the Man: The Life and Career of Lou Reed* (London: Omnibus Press, 2015)

Benjamin Moser, *Sontag: Her Life and Work* (New York: Ecco, 2019)

Simon Doonan (born 1952) is the author of many books including *Keith Haring, How to Be Yourself,* and *Drag: The Complete Story.* The former Barneys window dresser and creative ambassador is a style/culture commentator and an expert judge on the Emmy-nominated NBC series *Making It.* Simon lives in Florida with his partner, the ceramicist and designer Jonathan Adler, and their rescue mutt, Foxylady.